Wellesley Ontario in Colour Photos, Saving Our History One Photo at a Time

Photography
by Barbara Raué
2014

Series Name:
Cruising Ontario

Book 74: Wellesley

Cover photo: Nafziger Road

Series Name: Cruising Ontario
Saving Our History One Photo at a Time

Other Books by Barbara Raue

Coins of Gold

Arrows, Indians and Love

The Life and Times of Barbara
Volume 1: Inventions That Have Enhanced My Life
Volume 2: Entertainment That I Have Enjoyed
Volume 3: East Coast Trips
Volume 4: Olympics Have Always Intrigued Me
Volume 5: Wonders of the World
Volume 6: Caribbean Cruises We Have Enjoyed
Volume 7: Animals
Volume 8: Storms and Other Major Disasters in My Lifetime
Volume 9: Wars, Terrorist Attacks and Major Disasters

The Cromwell Family Book

Laura Secord Discovered

Visit Barbara's website to view all of her books
http://barbararaue.ericraue.com

The Township of Wellesley is the rural, north-western township of the Regional Municipality of Waterloo. The township comprises the communities of Bamberg, Crosshill, Hawkesville, Heidelberg, Kingwood, Knight's Corners, Linwood, Macton, St. Clements, Wallenstein and Wellesley.

The country scenery and rolling hills, along with its small town feel, have transformed the township into a commuter town with the population travelling into the nearby cities of Kitchener and Waterloo for work.

Wellesley Township was surveyed in 1842, but settlers were in this area long before. The town of Wellesley's original name was *Schmidtsville*, derived from its founding settler, John Schmidt. In 1851, the town was renamed *Wellesley* after Richard Wellesley, 1st Marquess Wellesley, the eldest brother of Arthur Wellesley, 1st Duke of Wellington. The community quickly grew to be the largest economic centre in rural Waterloo Region with a wood mill, feed mill, grain mill (which still stands after being constructed in 1856), leather tanner, cheese factory, restaurants and housing, and many other businesses that also brought much trade to the town from the nearby farms and farming villages.

When the Waterloo County boundaries were established in 1852 they included the townships of Waterloo, Wellesley, Wilmot, Woolwich, and North Dumfries.

The first library in Wellesley Village was incorporated in 1900. The current branch is located in the former S.S. No. 16 Wellesley Township public school building. The school closed its doors in 1967.

Table of Contents

Wellesley

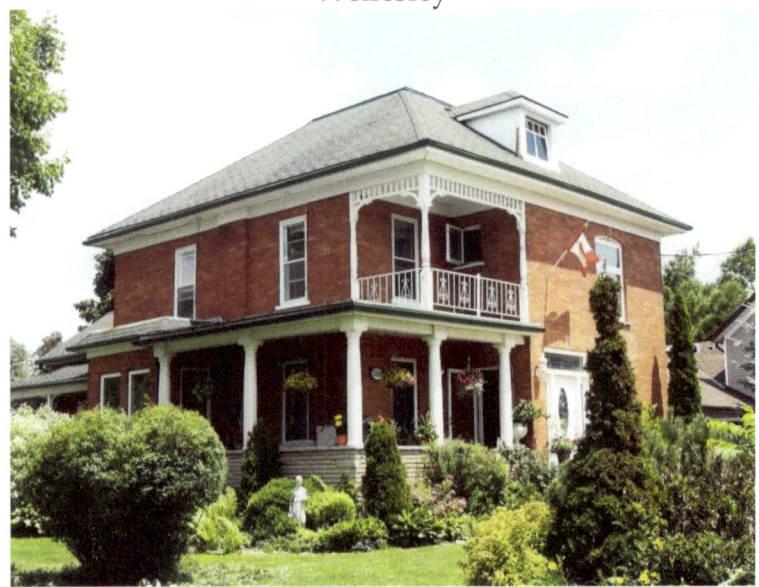

1115 Queen's Bush Road – Italianate style, hipped roof, dormer

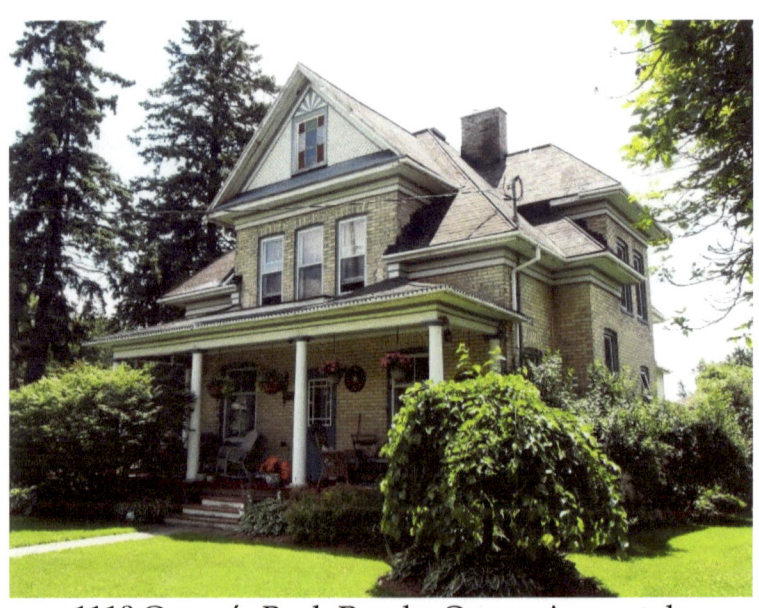

1110 Queen's Bush Road – Queen Anne style

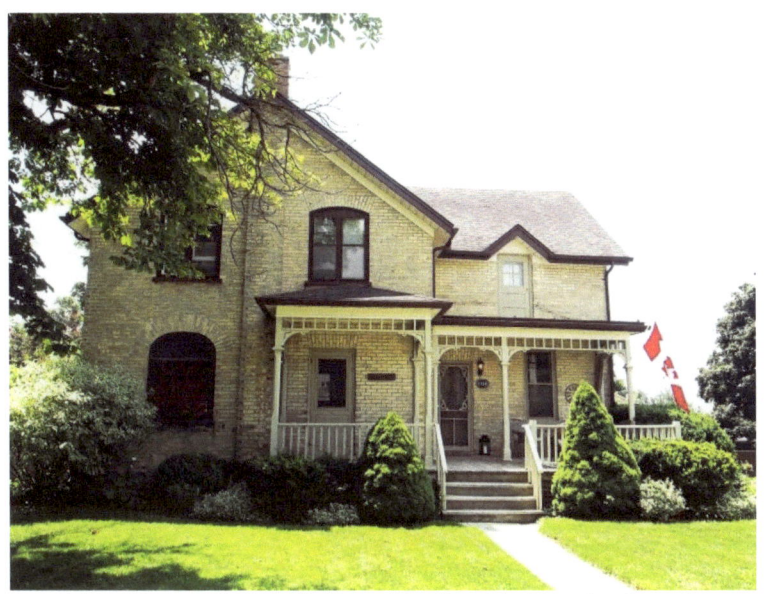

1116 Queen's Bush Road – Gothic Revival style

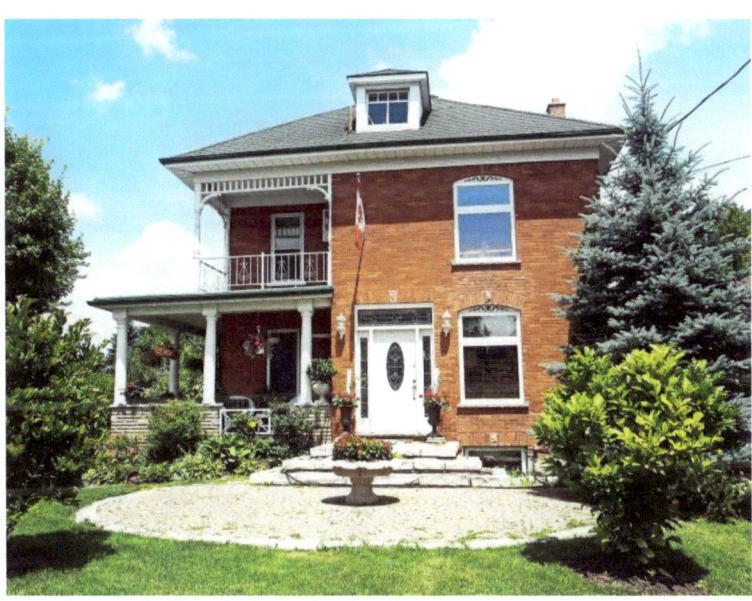

Queen's Bush Road – Italianate, dormer in attic,
Second floor balcony

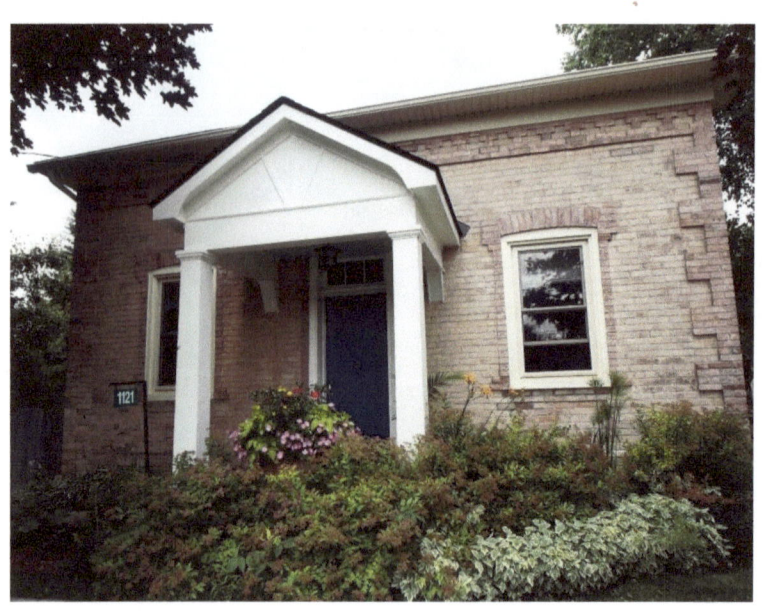

1121 Queen's Bush Road

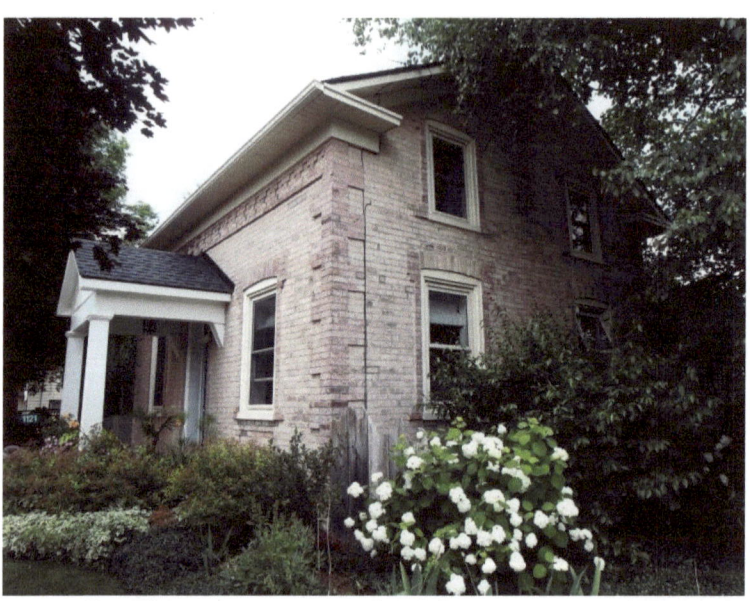

Cornice return on end gable, corner quoins

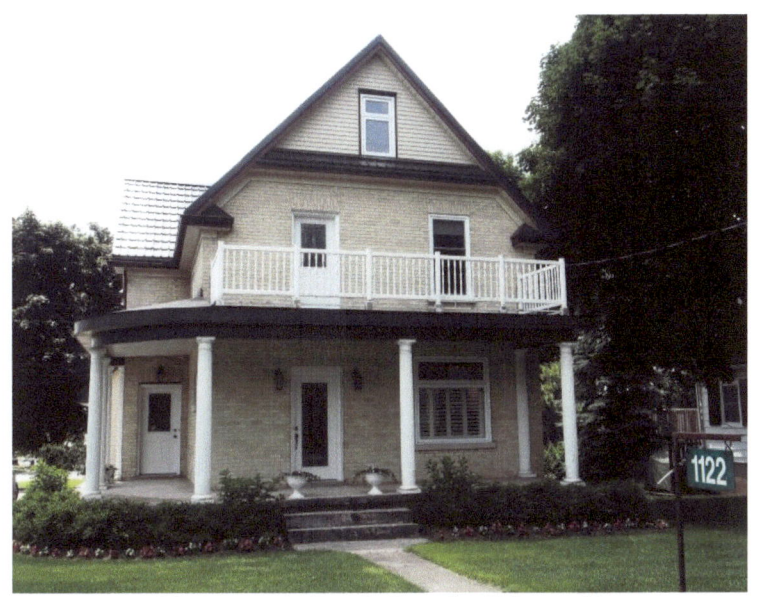

1122 Queen's Bush Road - Edwardian

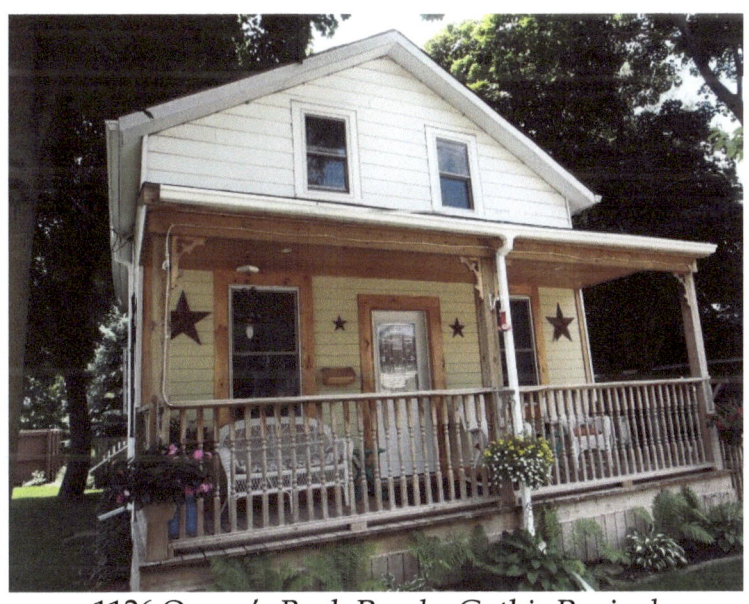

1126 Queen's Bush Road – Gothic Revival

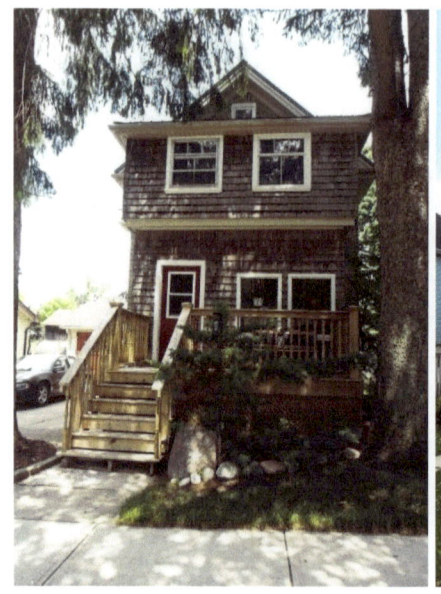

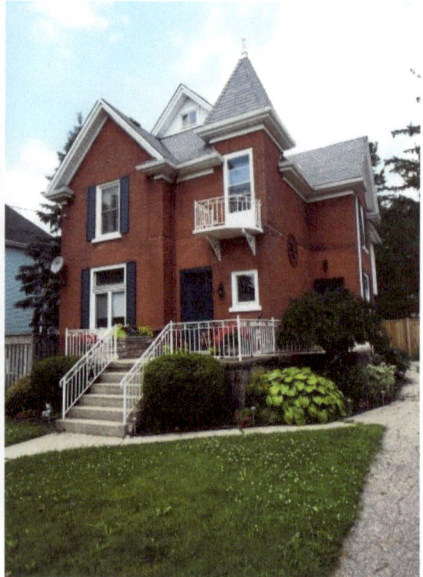

Gothic Revival

1155 Queen's Bush Road
Queen Anne style

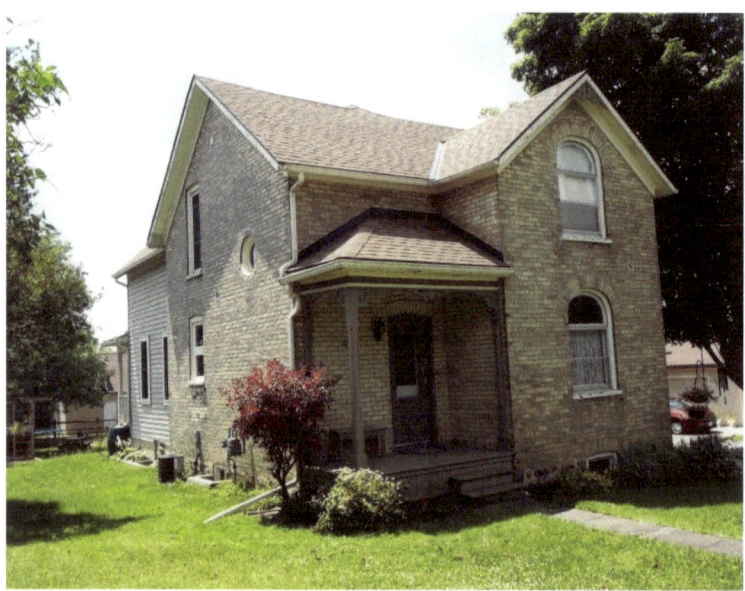

1134 Queen's Bush Road – Gothic Revival, yellow brick

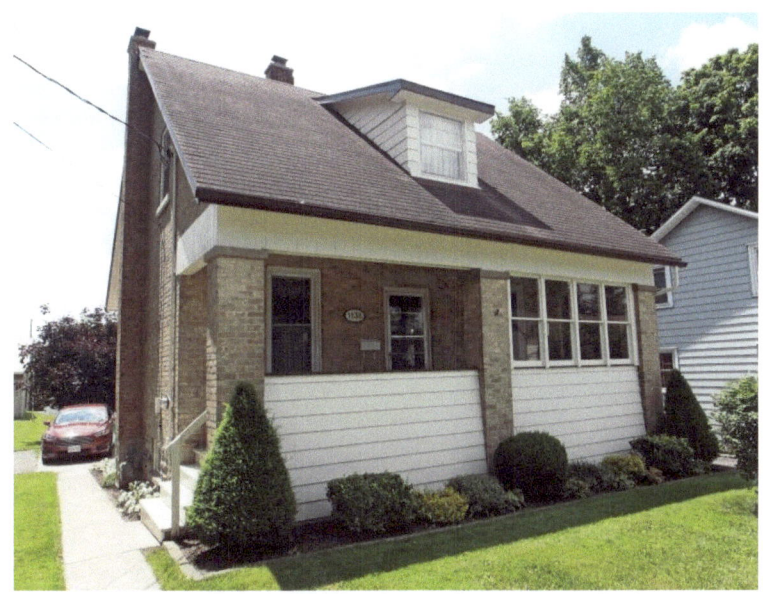

1138 Queen's Bush Road, Gothic Revival, dormer

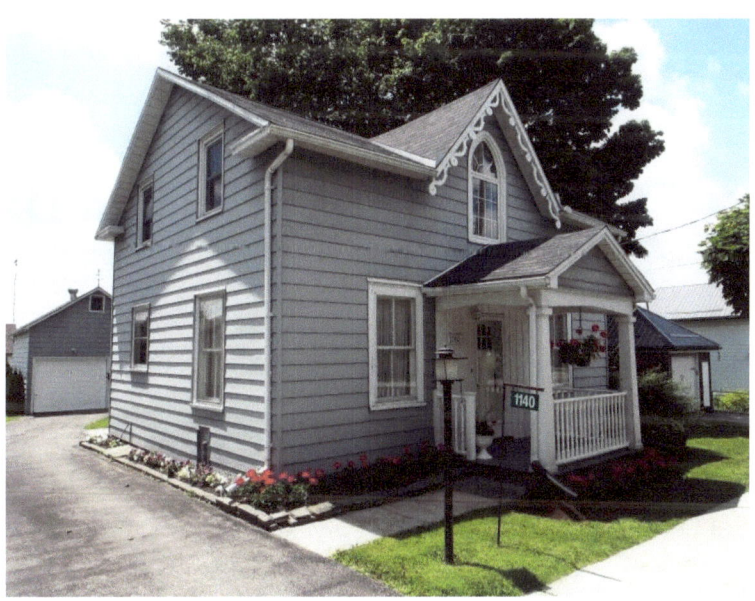

1140 Queen's Bush Road – Gothic Revival,
Vergeboard trim on gable

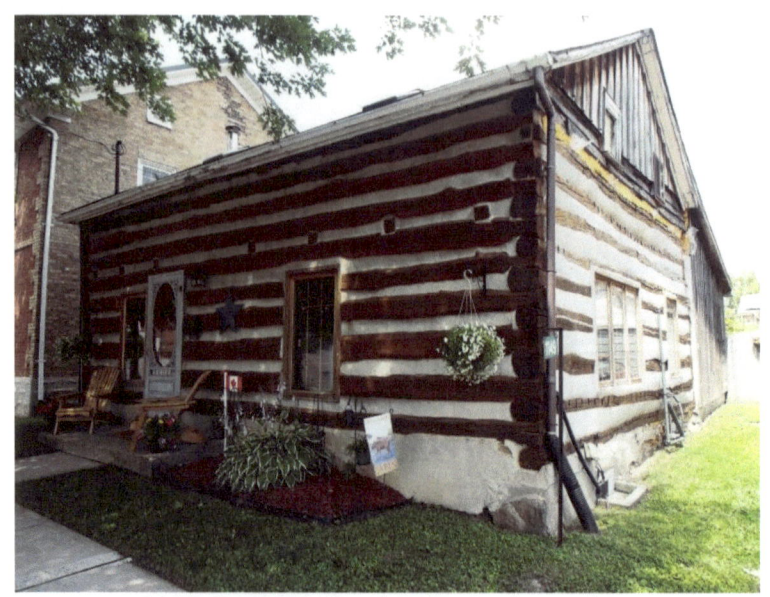

1149 Queen's Bush Road – log cabin

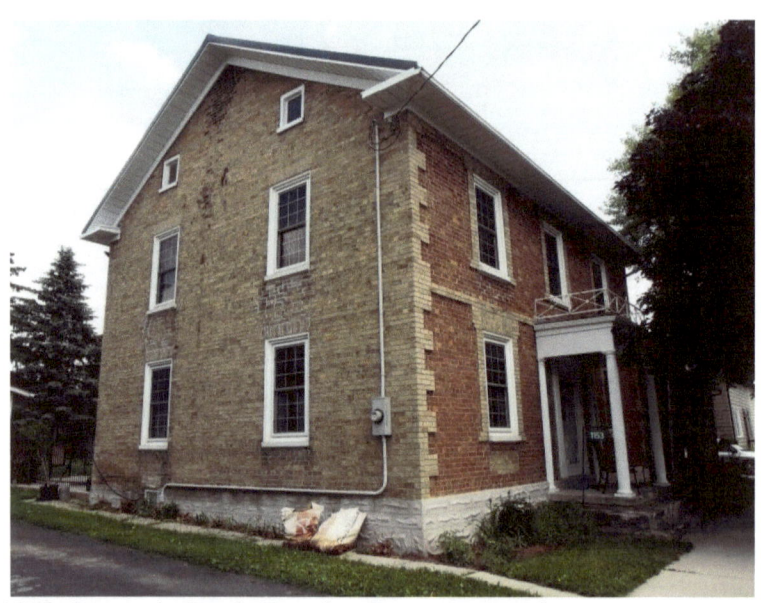

1153 Queen's Bush Road – Georgian style, corner quoins

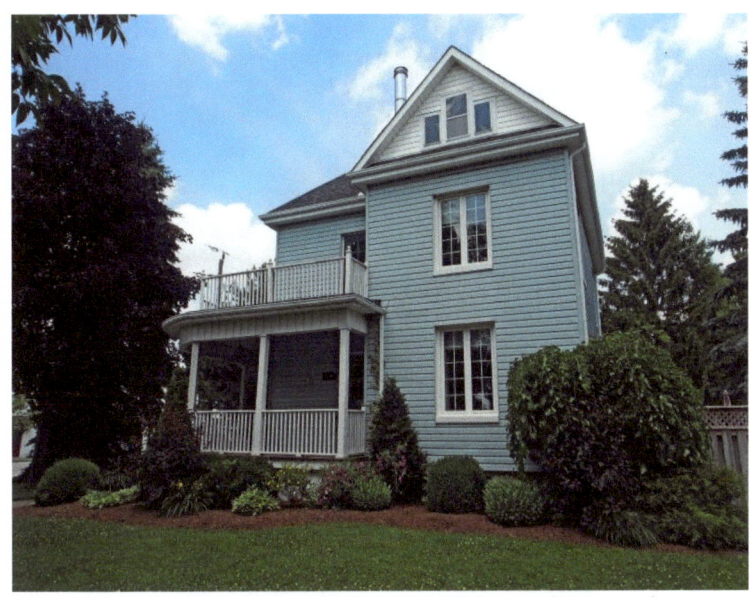

1159 Queen's Bush Road – Edwardian style,
Palladian window, second floor balcony

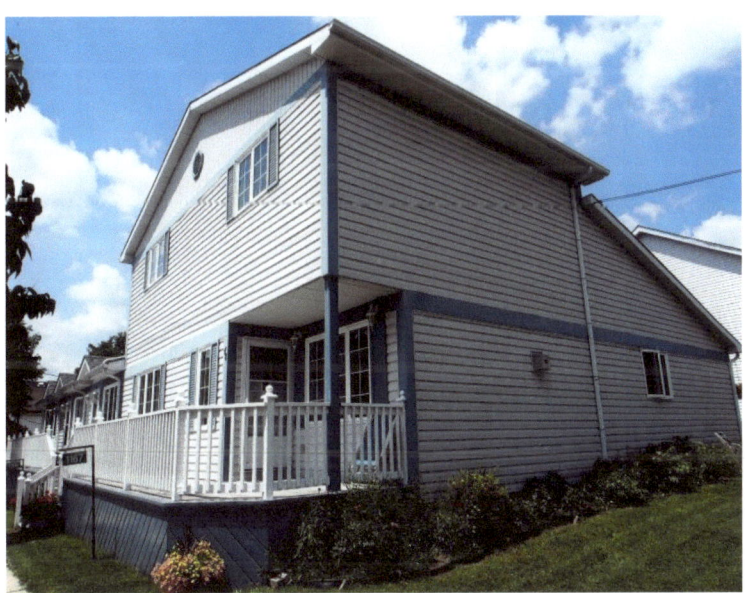

1167 Queen's Bush Road

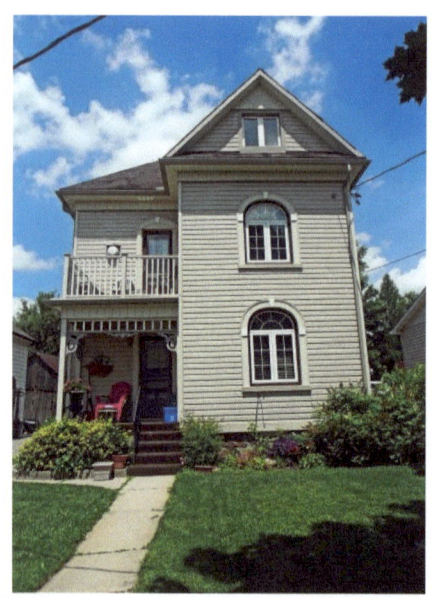

1175 Queen's Bush Road - Edwardian

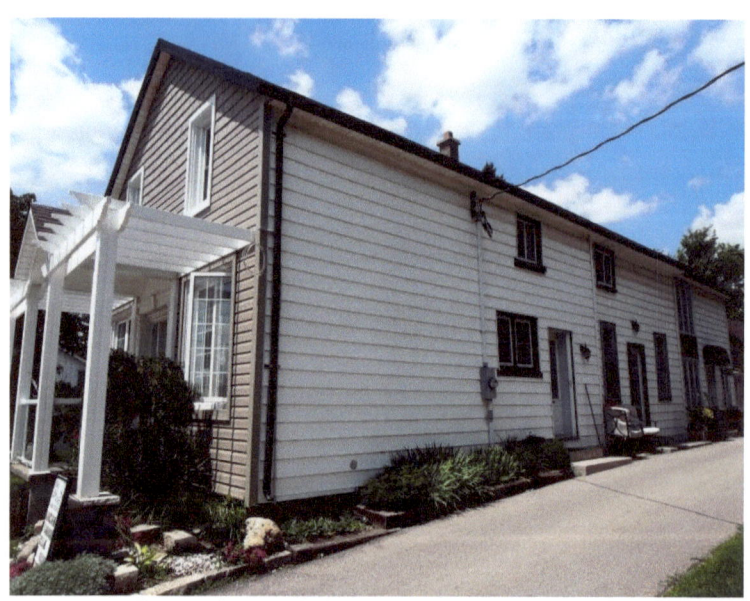

Queen's Bush Road – Gothic Revival

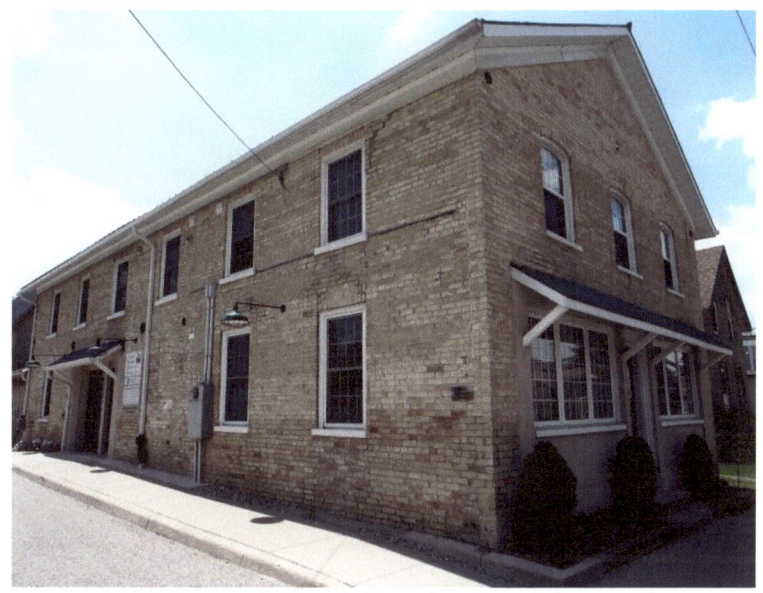

1180 Queen's Bush Road – Georgian style

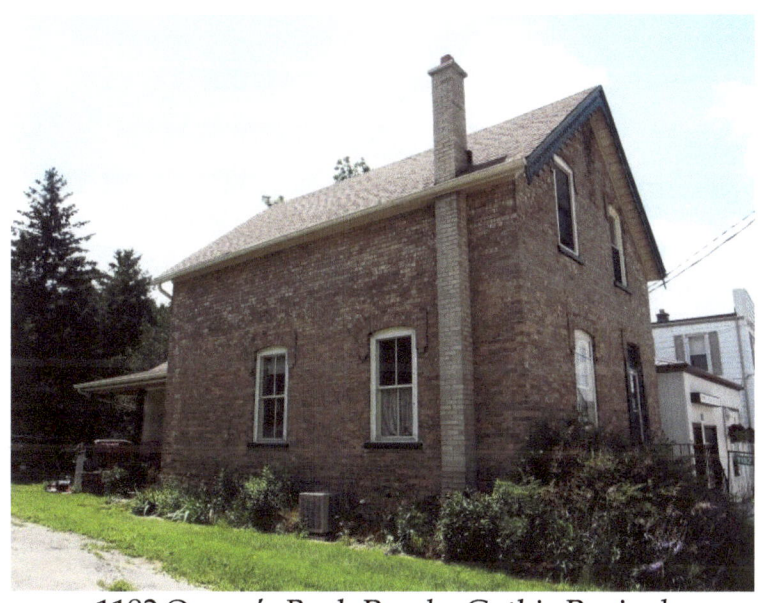

1182 Queen's Bush Road – Gothic Revival

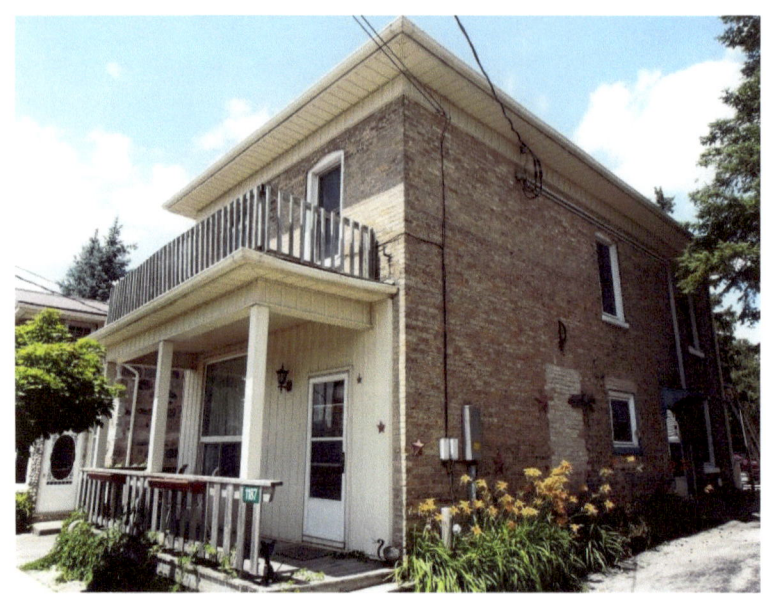

1187 Queen's Bush Road – Italianate, second floor balcony

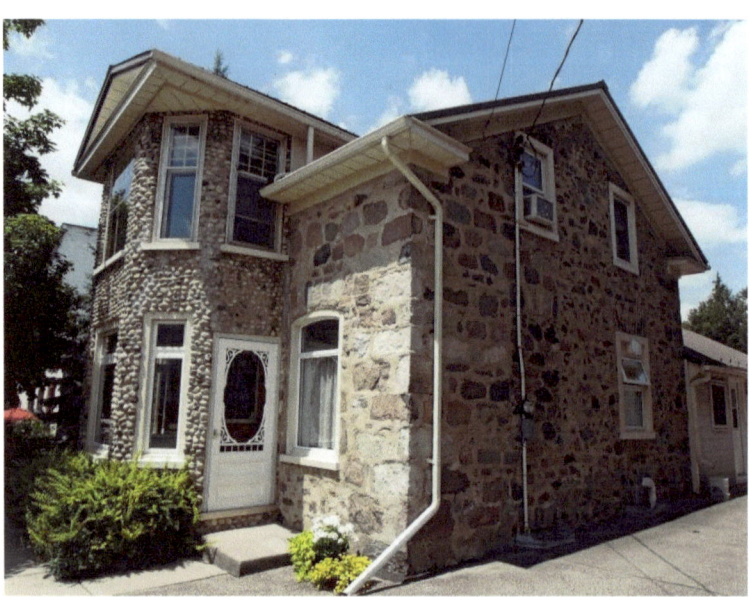

1189 Queen's Bush Road – cobblestone architecture,
Cornice return on end gable

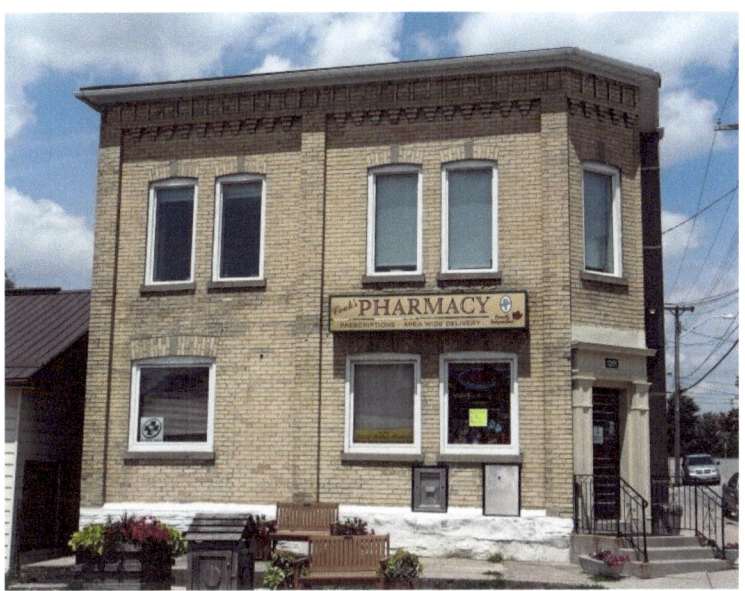

1201 Queen's Bush Road – Italianate, dentil moulding

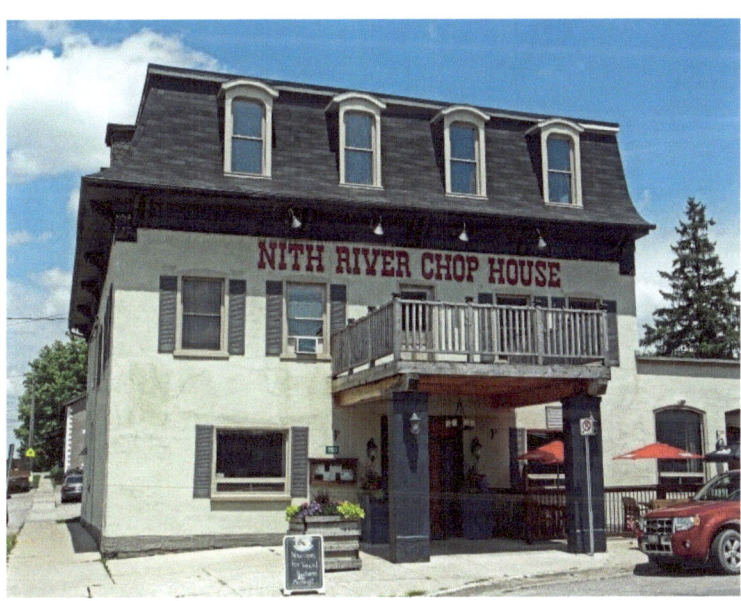

1193 Queen's Bush Road – Nith River Chop House
Second Empire style – mansard roof with dormers

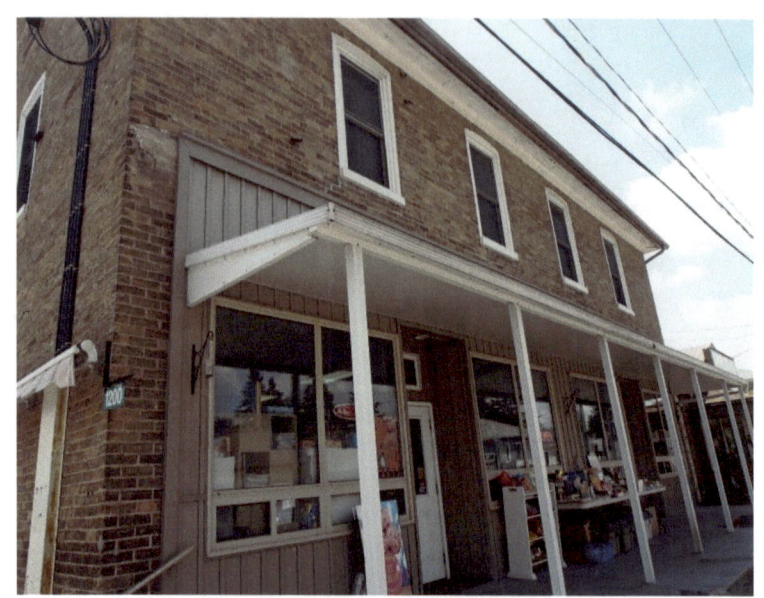

1200 Queen's Bush Road

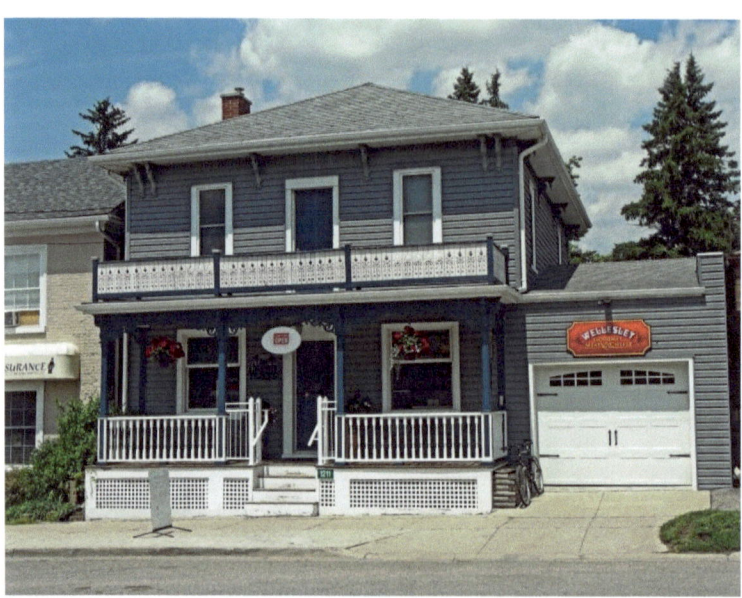

1211 Queen's Bush Road – Italianate, cornice brackets,
Second floor balcony

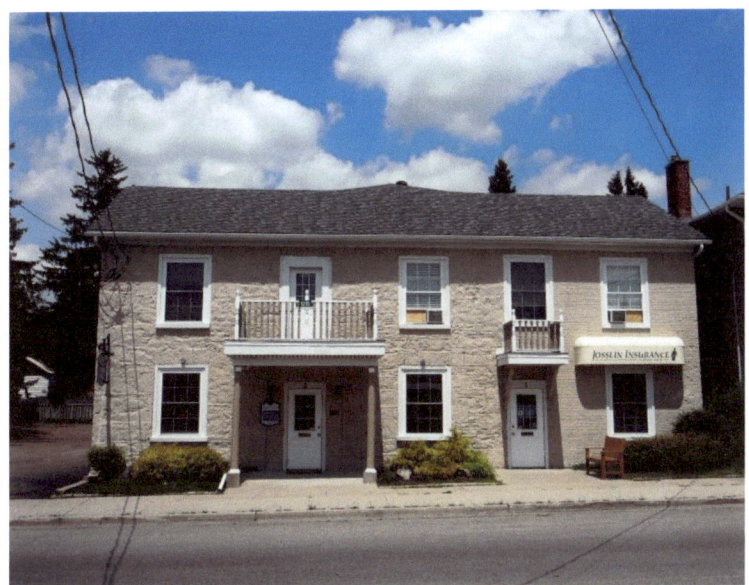

1215 Queen's Bush Road

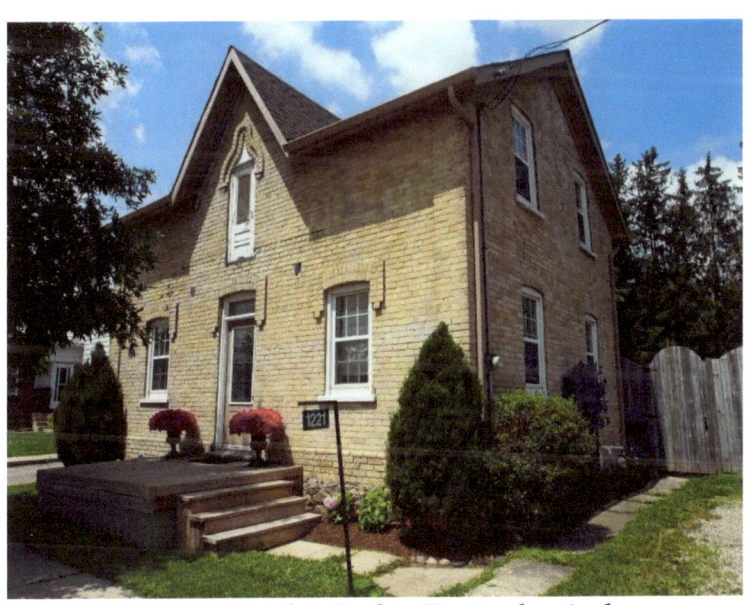

1221 Queen's Bush Road – Gothic Revival, window voussoirs

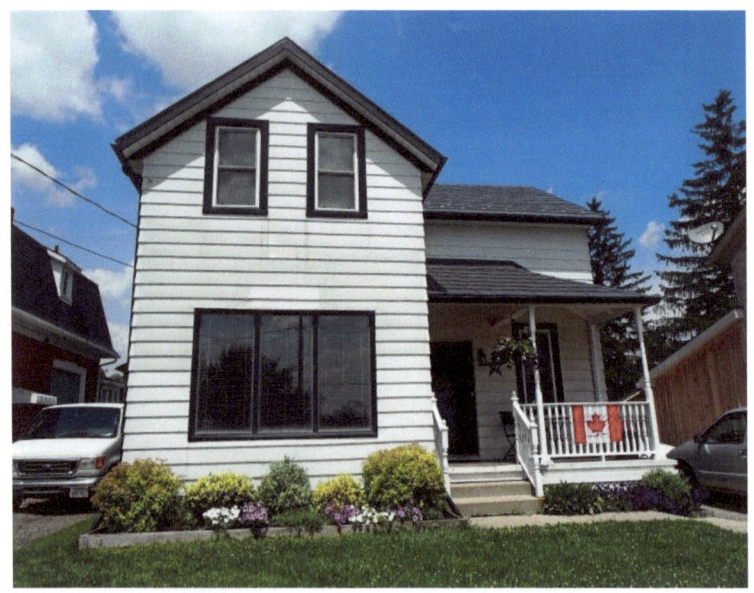

1223 Queen's Bush Road - Gothic

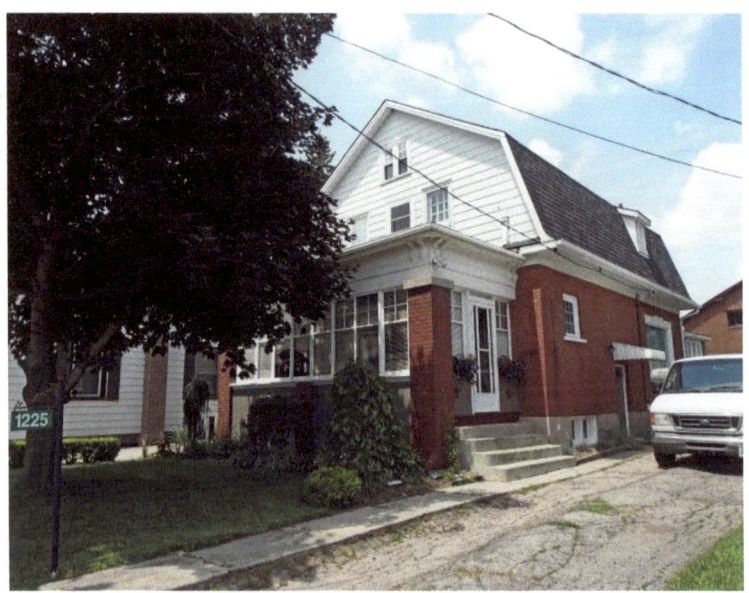

1225 Queen's Bush Road

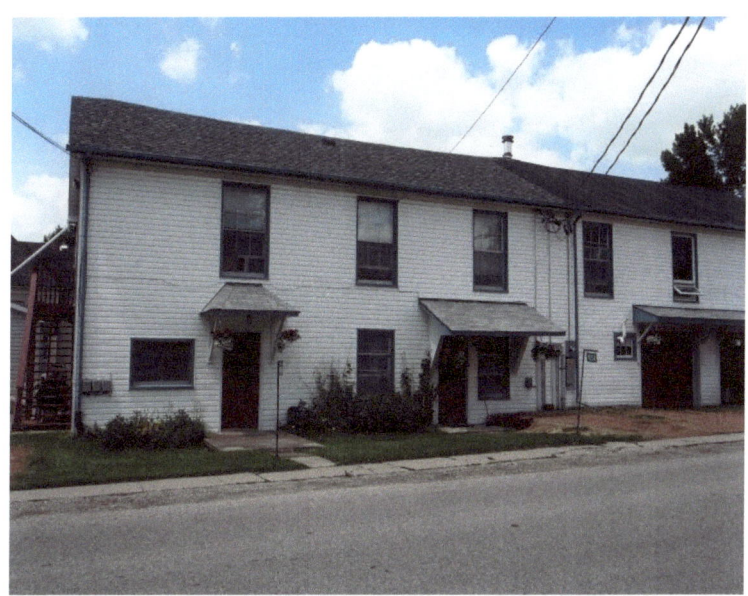

1056-1058 Molesworth Street

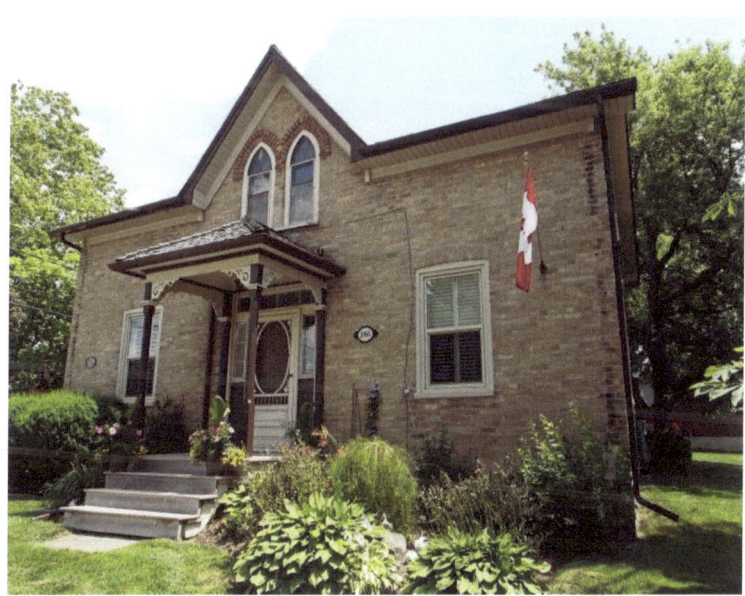

1065 Molesworth Street – Buxton House – Gothic Revival
Twin lancet windows in centre gable

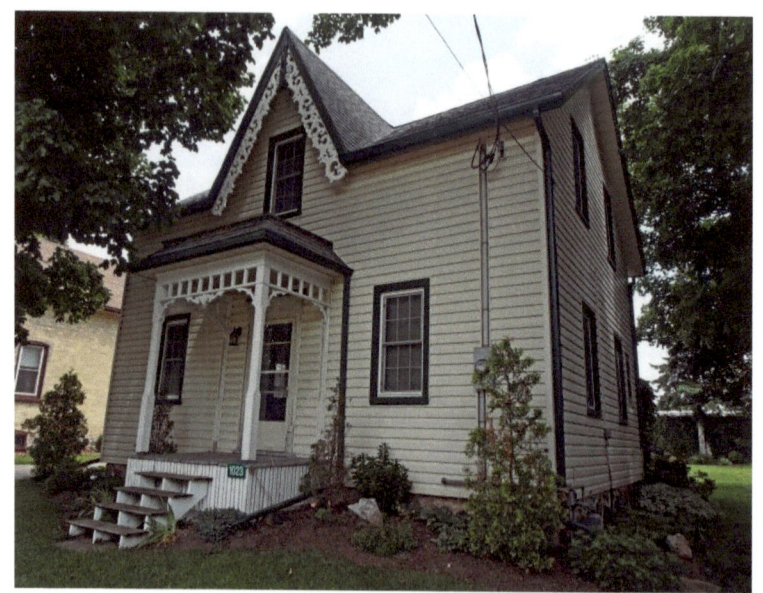

1023 Molesworth Street – Gothic Revival, Vergeboard trim

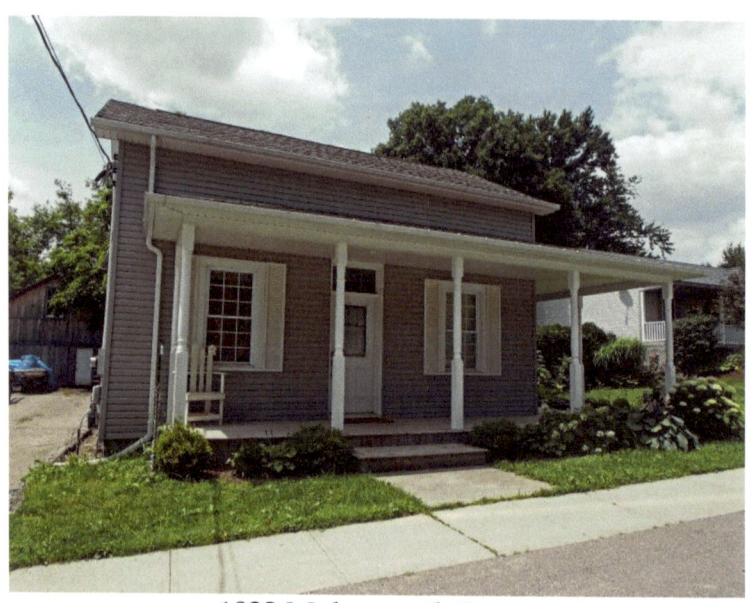

1022 Molesworth Street

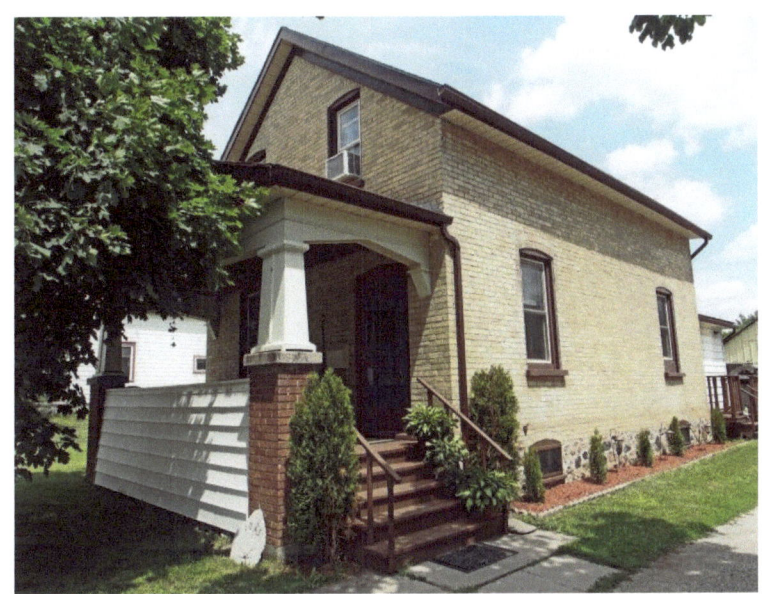

1025 Molesworth Street – Gothic Revival

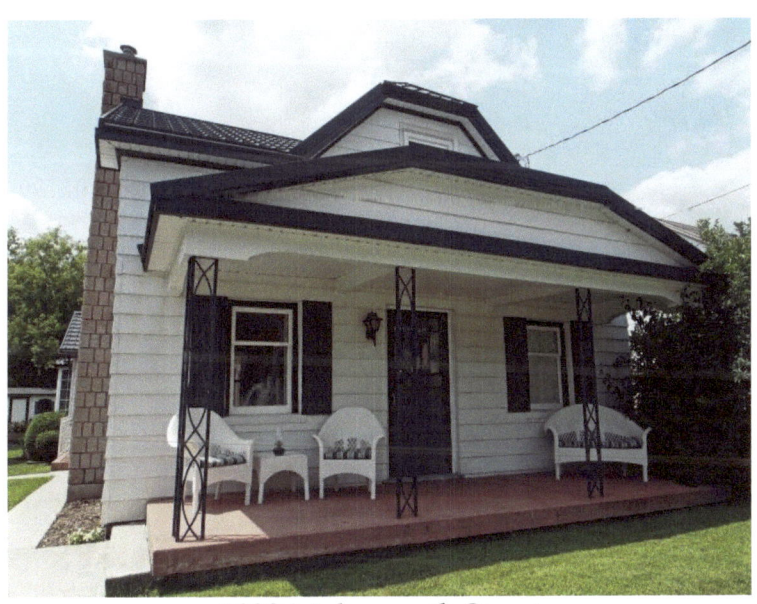

1032 Molesworth Street

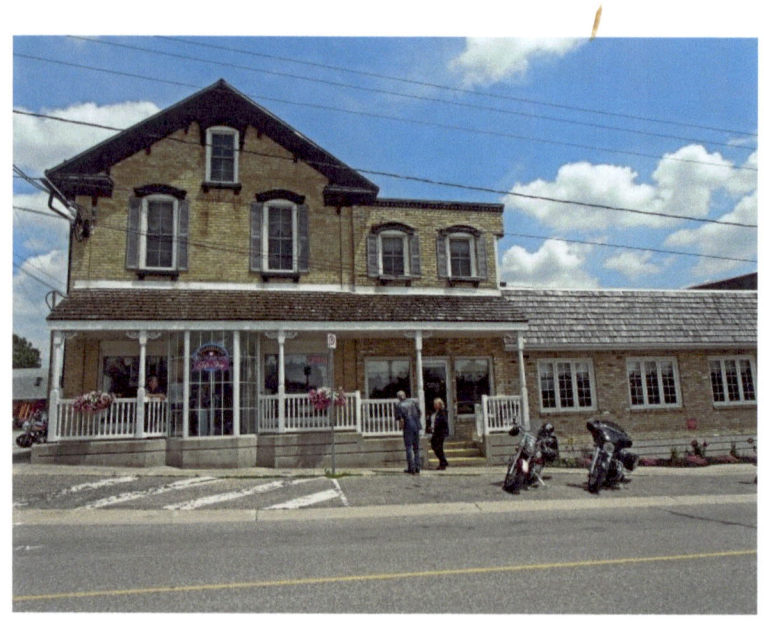

Molesworth Street – Schmidtsville Restaurant

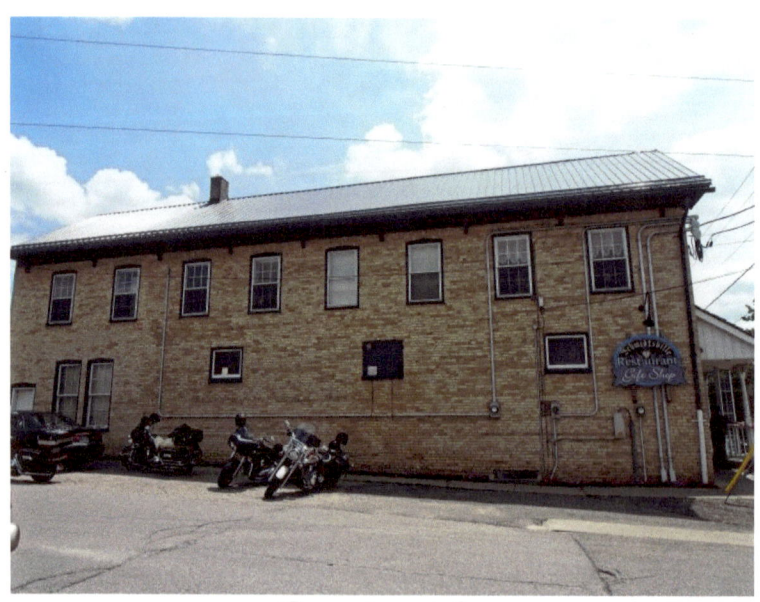

Georgian style

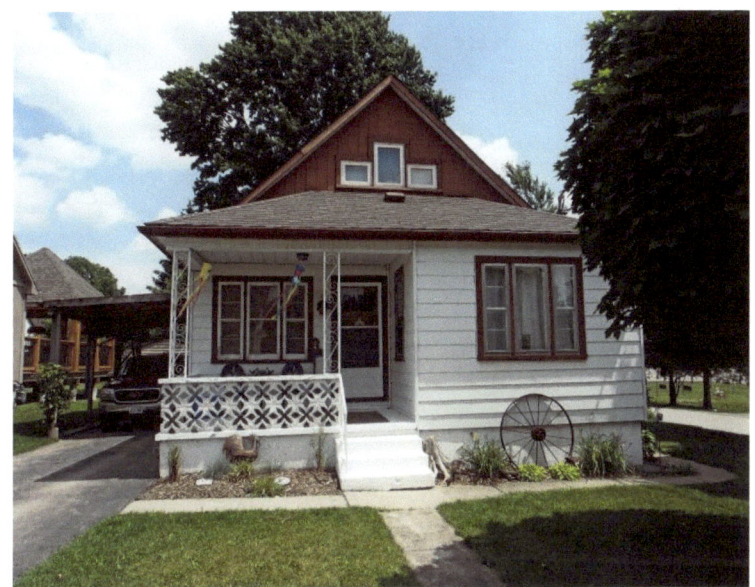

1037 Molesworth Street – Gothic Revival, Palladian window

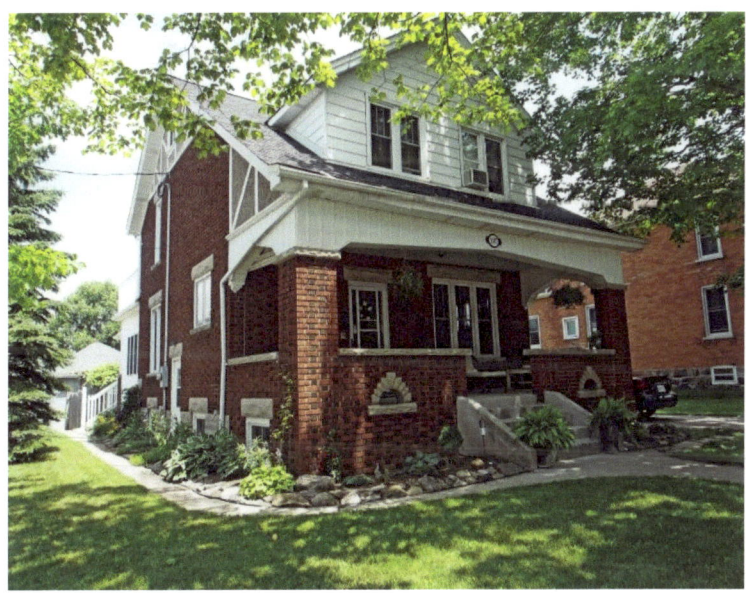

1107 Henry Street – cobblestone basement

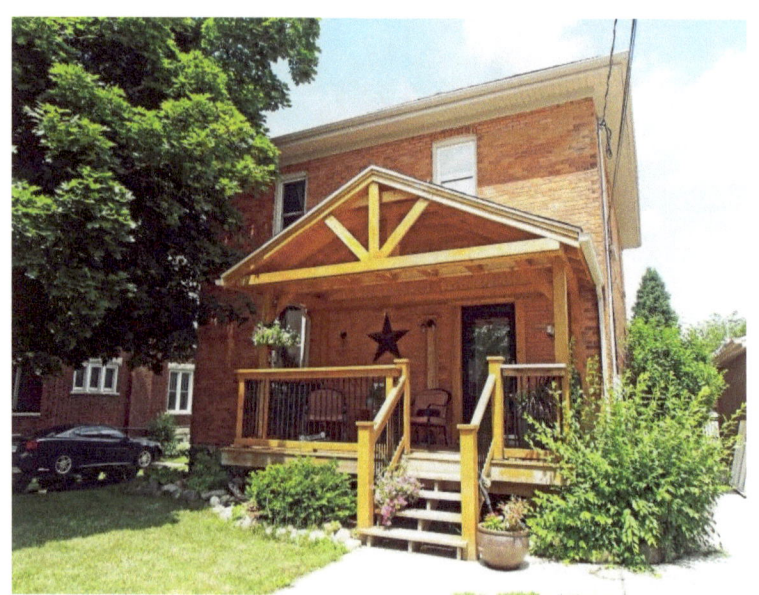

1101 Henry Street - Italianate

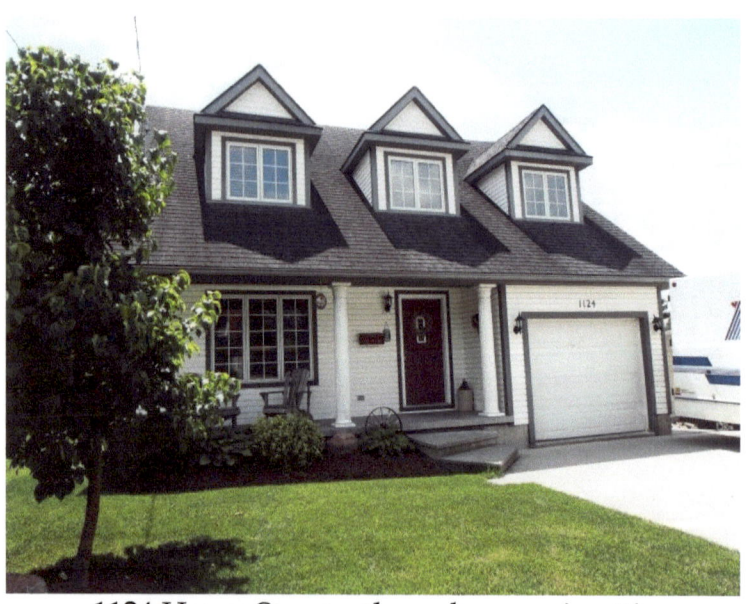

1124 Henry Street – three dormers in attic

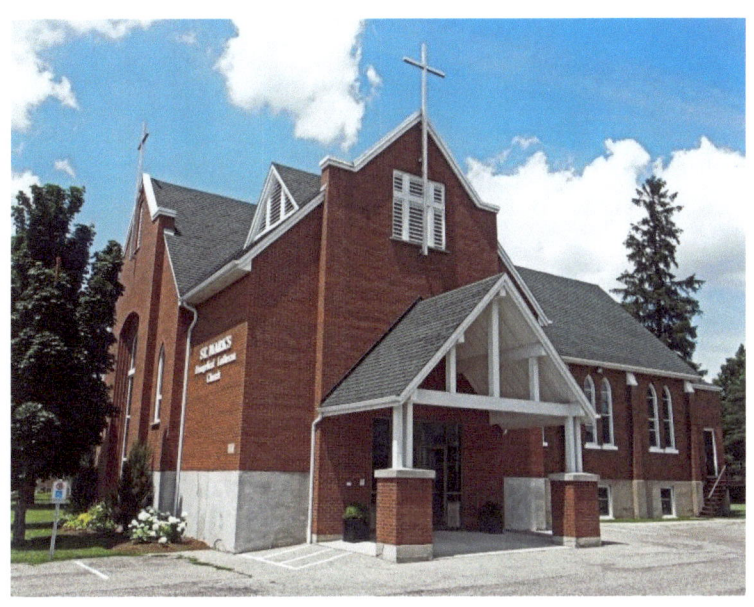

Henry Street - St. Mark's Evangelical Lutheran Church
c. 1898

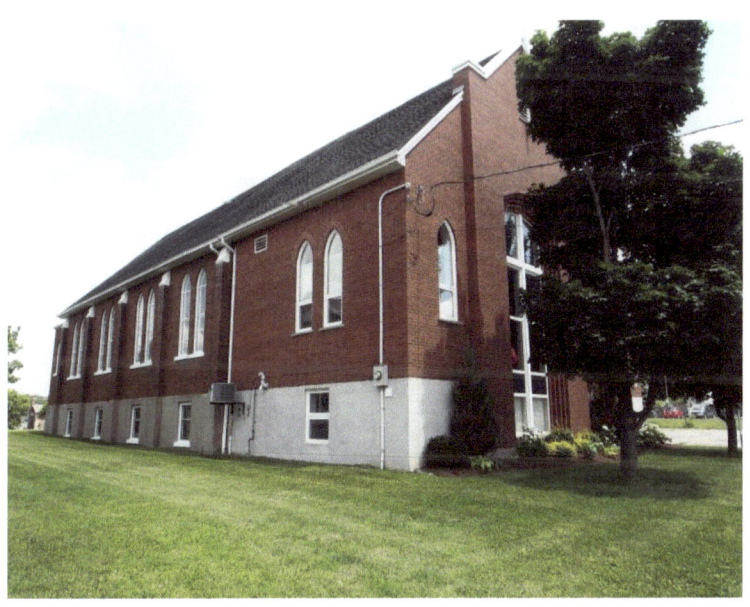

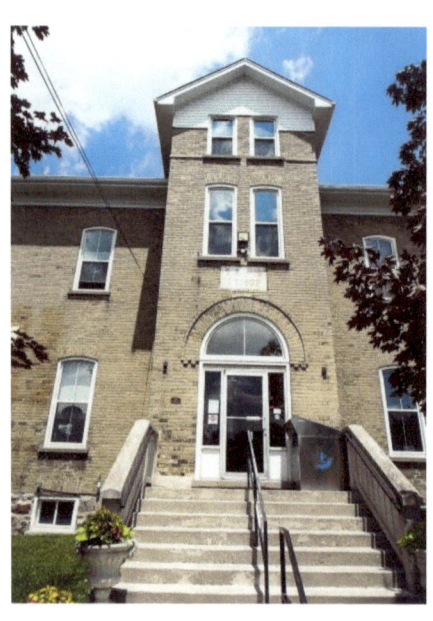

Henry Street – Wellesley Township Heritage Historical
Society – Italianate, hipped roof,
two-and-a-half storey tower-like frontispiece

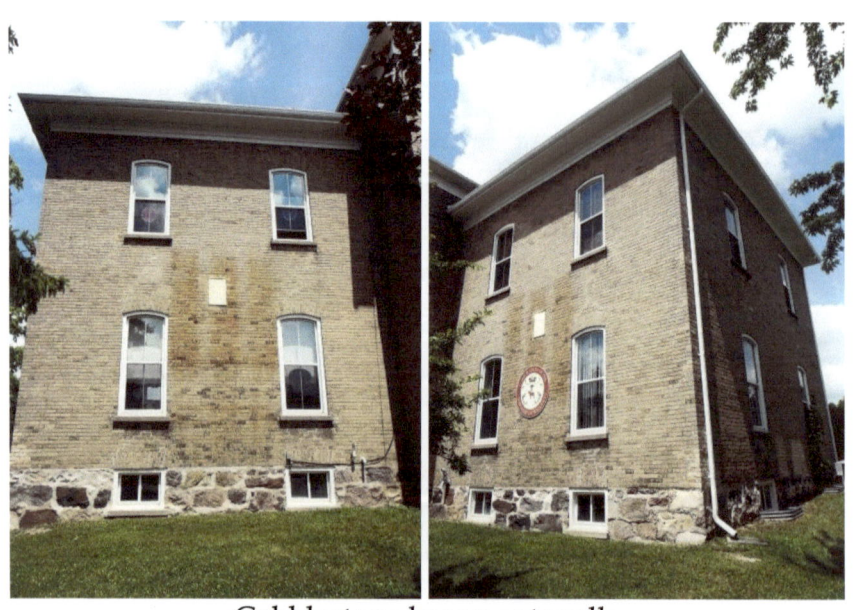

Cobblestone basement walls

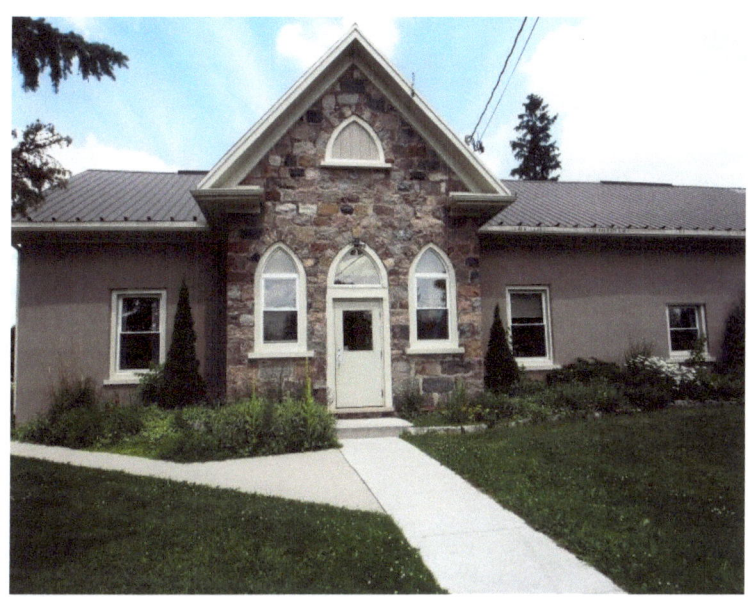

1129 Henry Street – Gothic Revival – cobblestone frontispiece, cornice return on gable

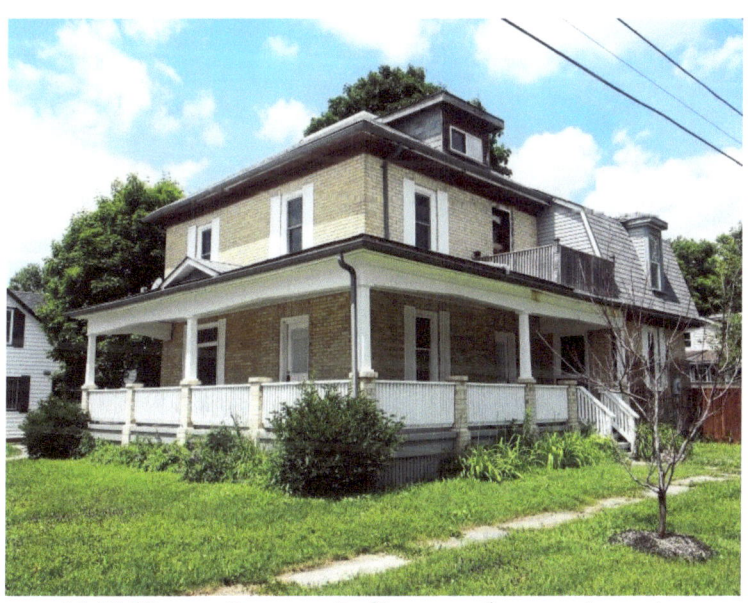

1147 Henry Street – Italianate, dormer in attic, wrap-around verandah

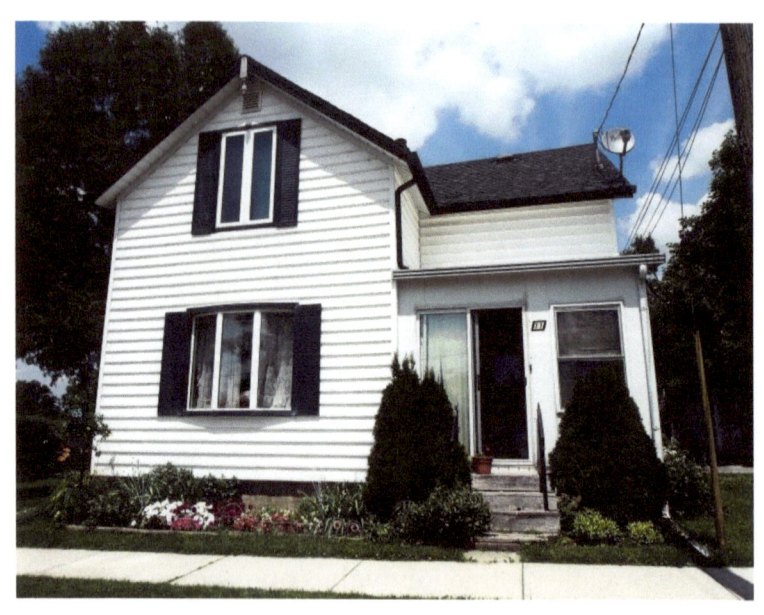

Henry Street – Gothic Revival

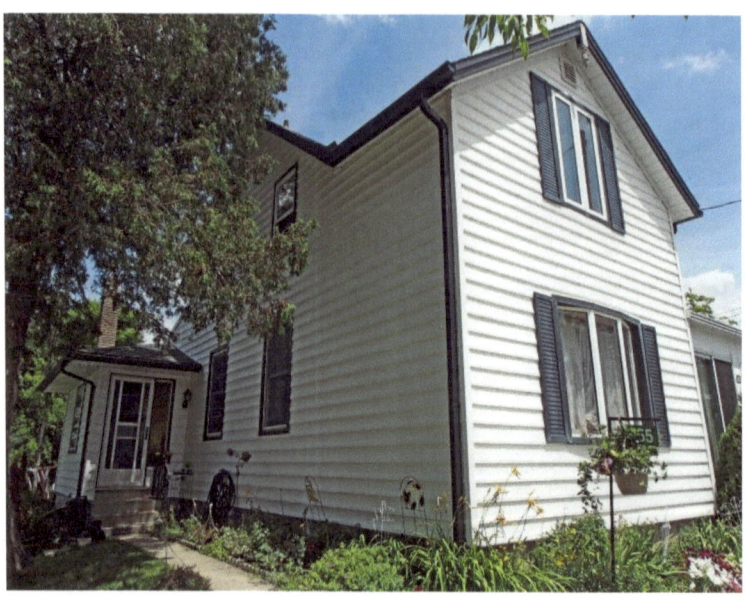

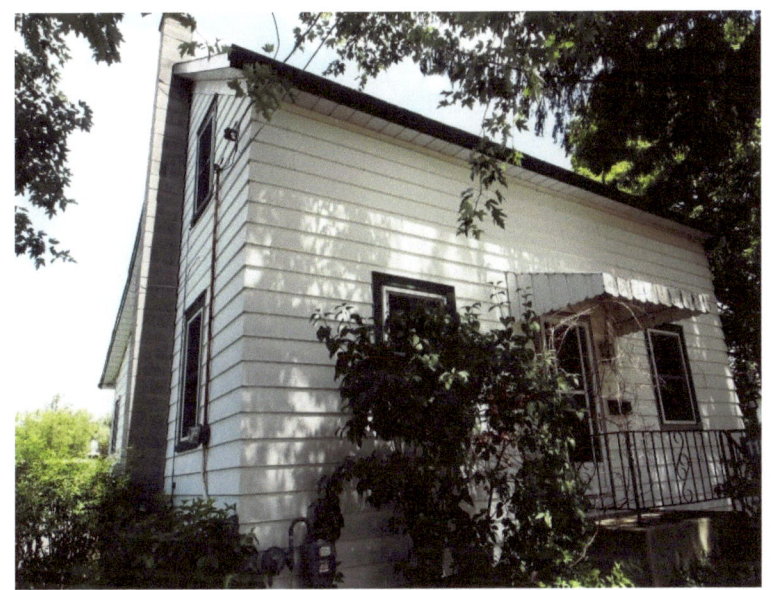

Henry Street

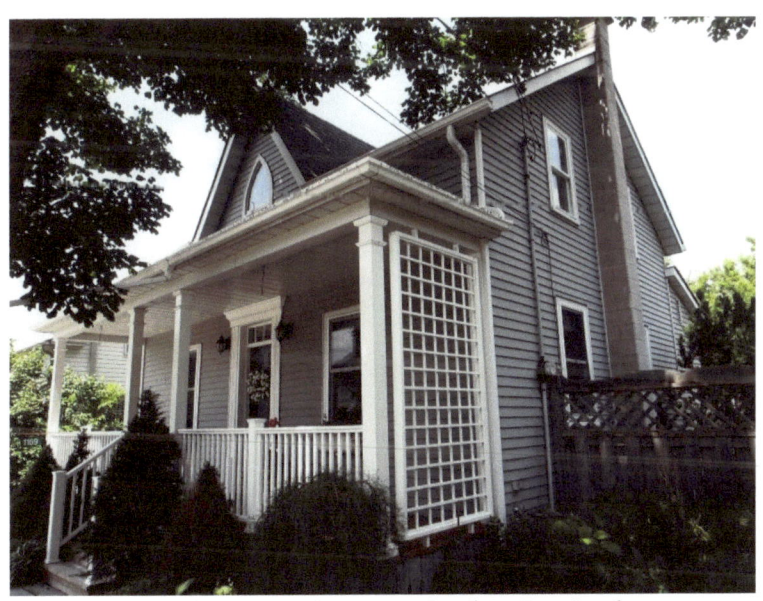

1169 Henry Street – Gothic Revival

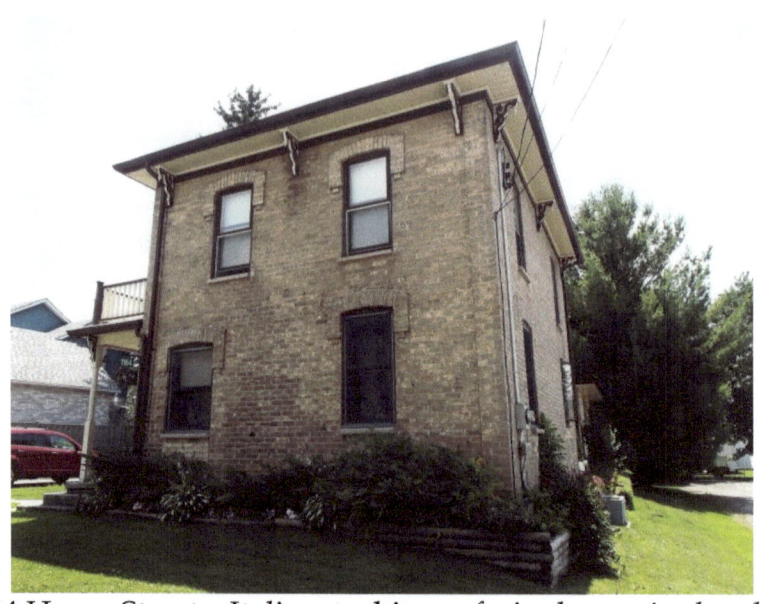

1164 Henry Street – Italianate, hip roof, single cornice brackets
Yellow brick, arched window voussoirs

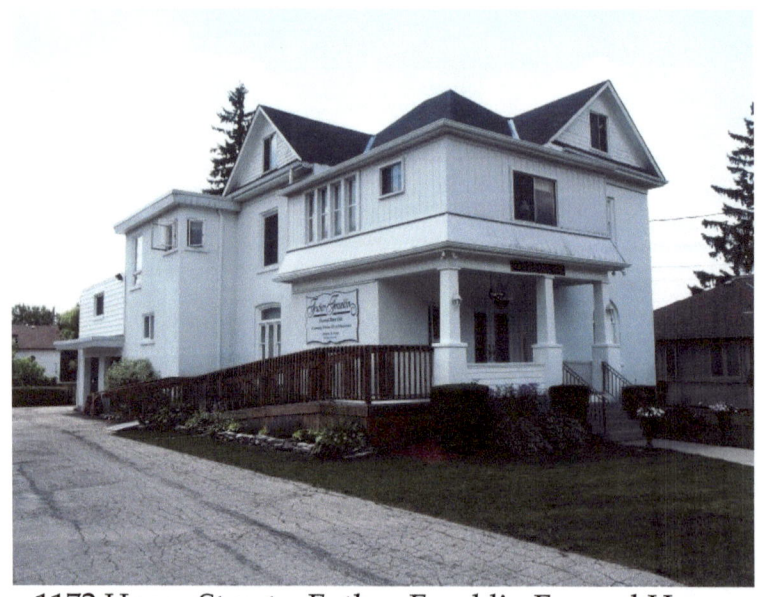

1172 Henry Street – Futher-Franklin Funeral Home

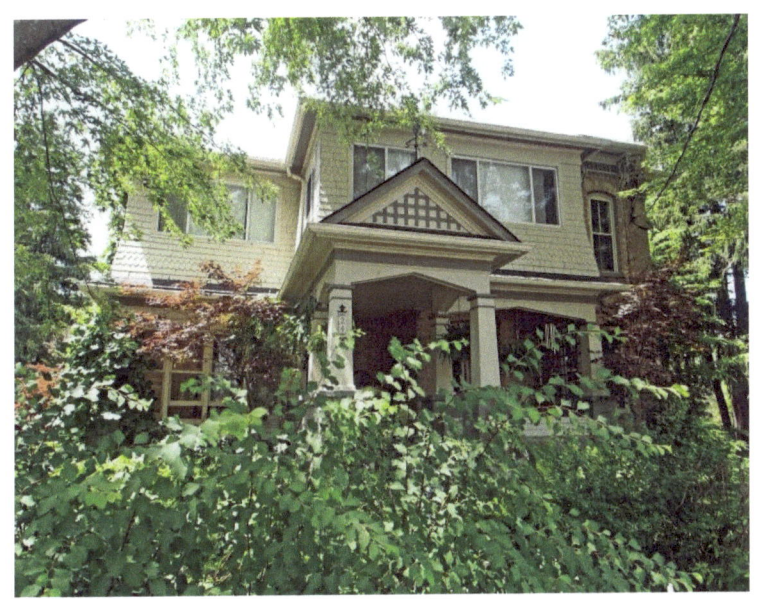

Henry Street – pediment above entranceway

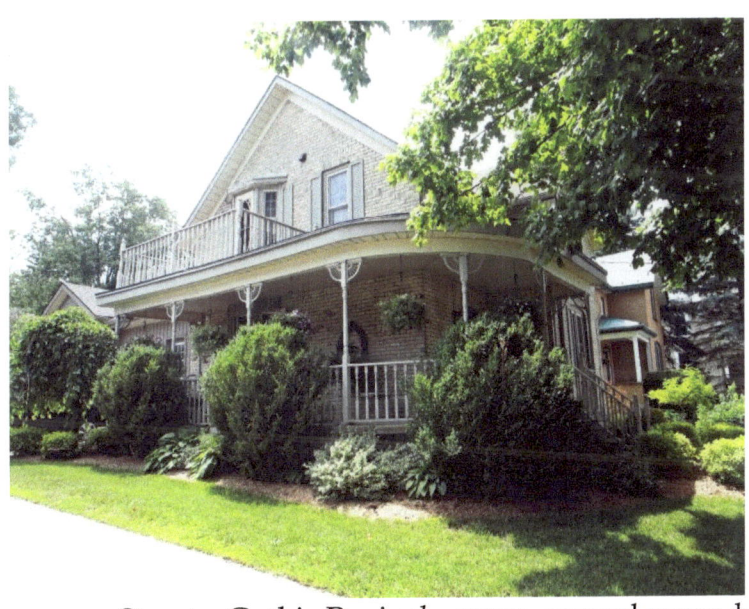

Lawrence Street – Gothic Revival – wrap-around verandah

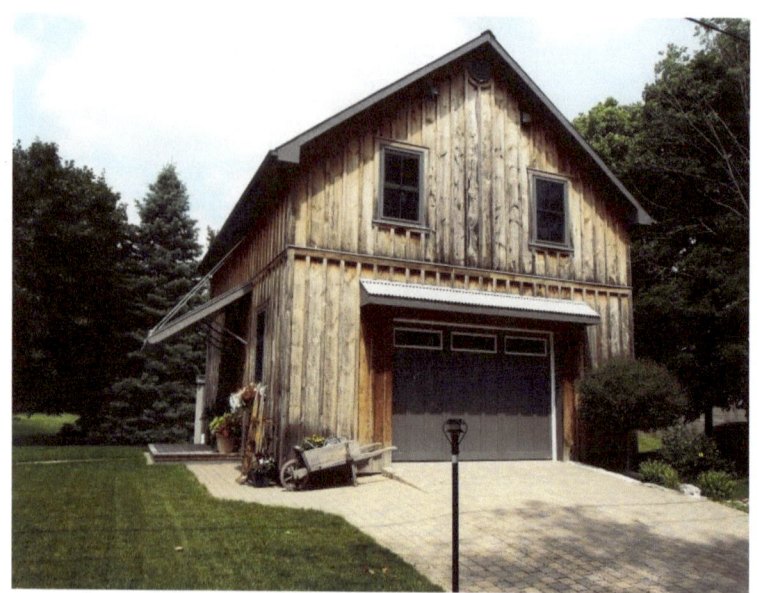

Lawrence Street

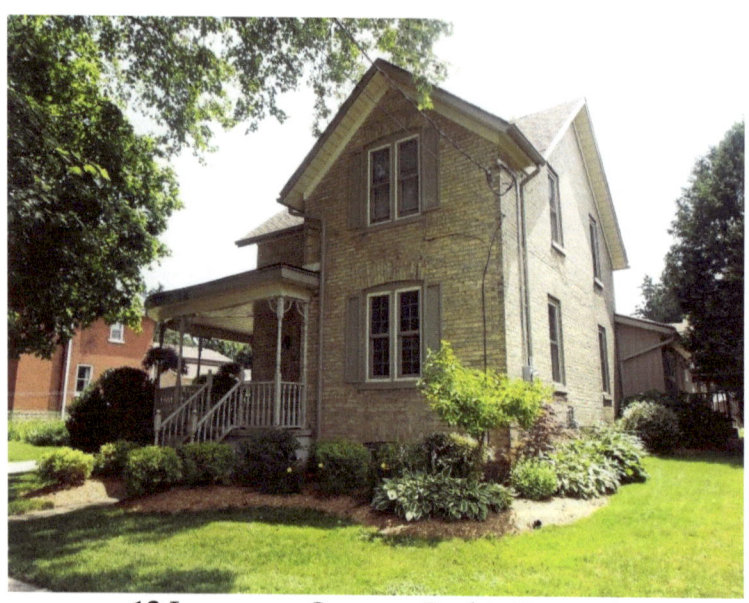

12 Lawrence Street – Gothic Revival

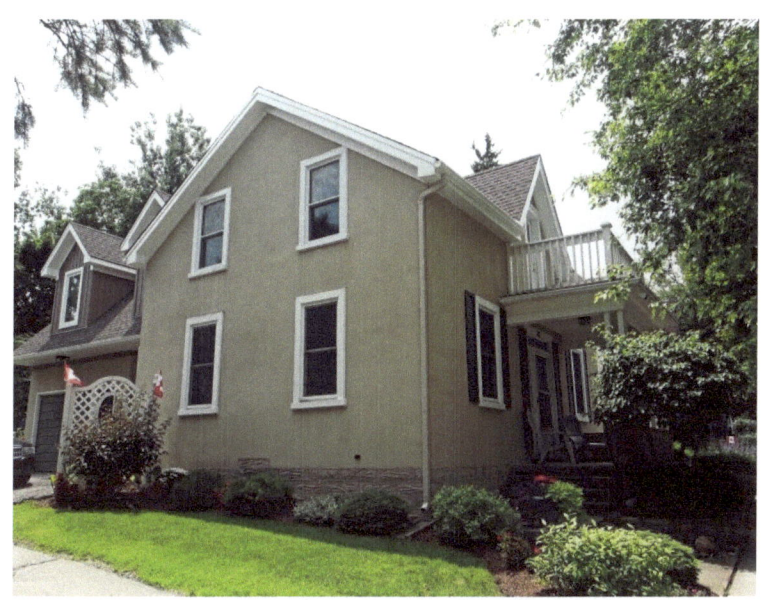

Lawrence Street – Gothic Revival
– updated with plaster siding

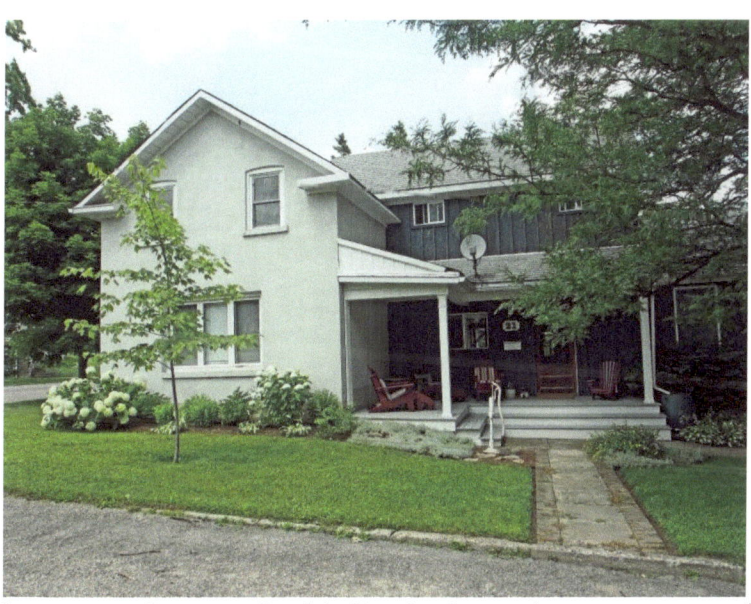

21 Lawrence Street – Gothic Revival, cornice return on gable

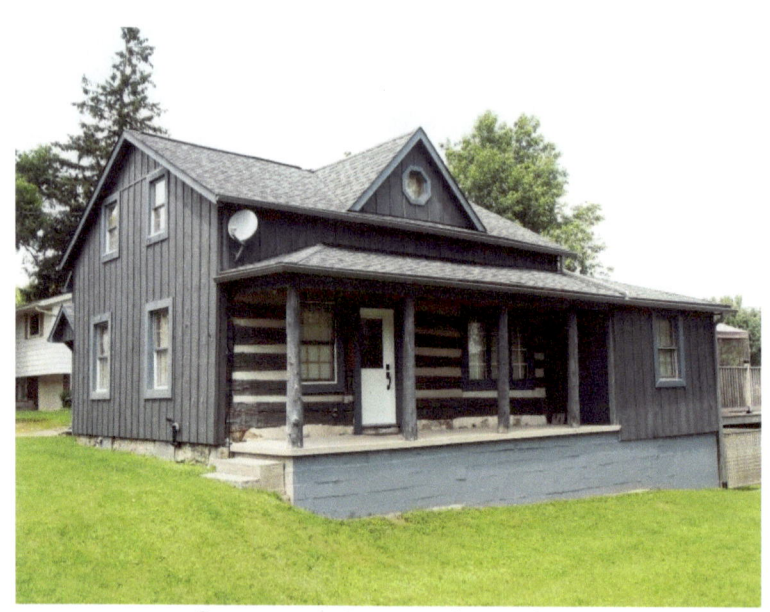

Lawrence Street – log cabin

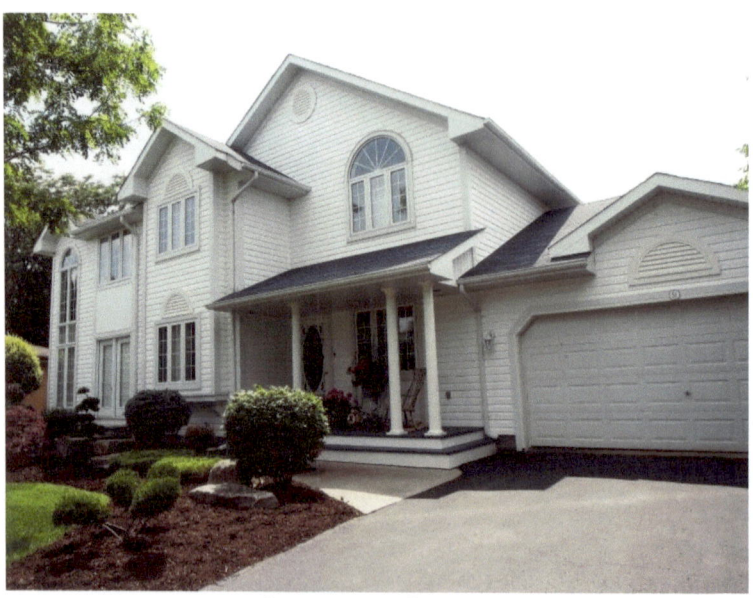

Lawrence Street

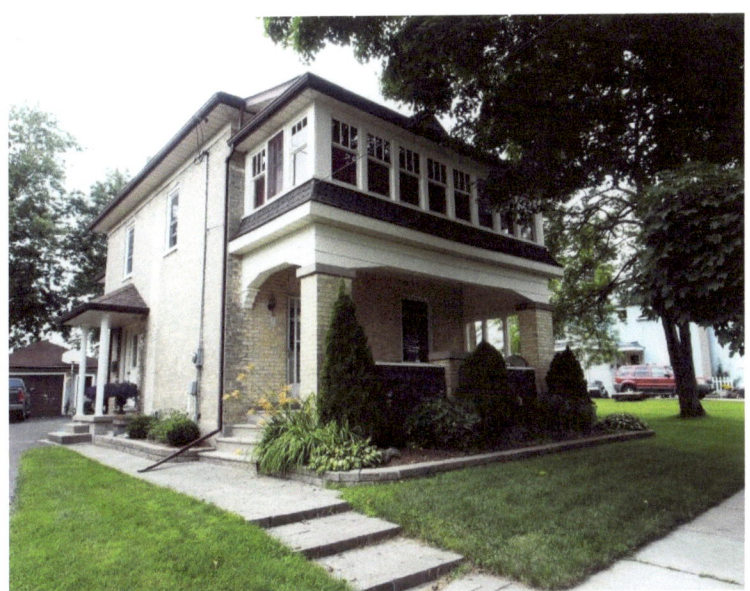

31 Lawrence Street – Italianate, hipped roof, enclosed
sunporch above verandah

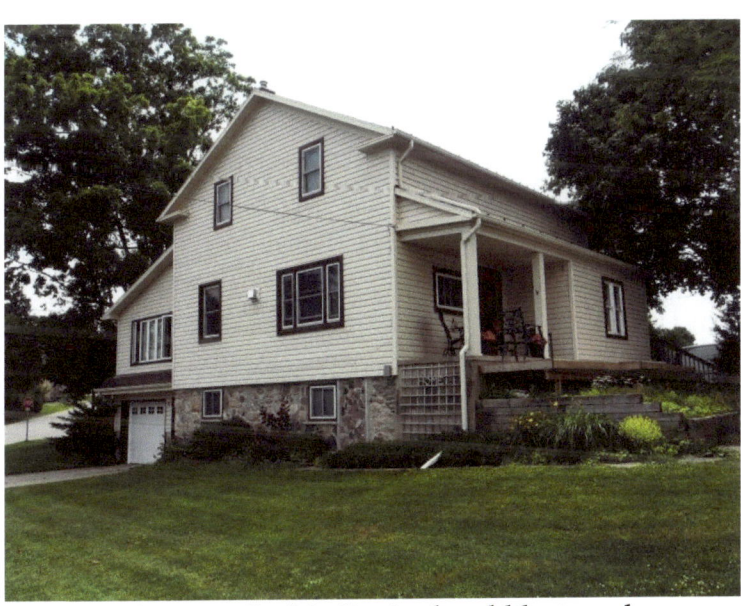

Lawrence Street – Gothic Revival, cobblestone basement

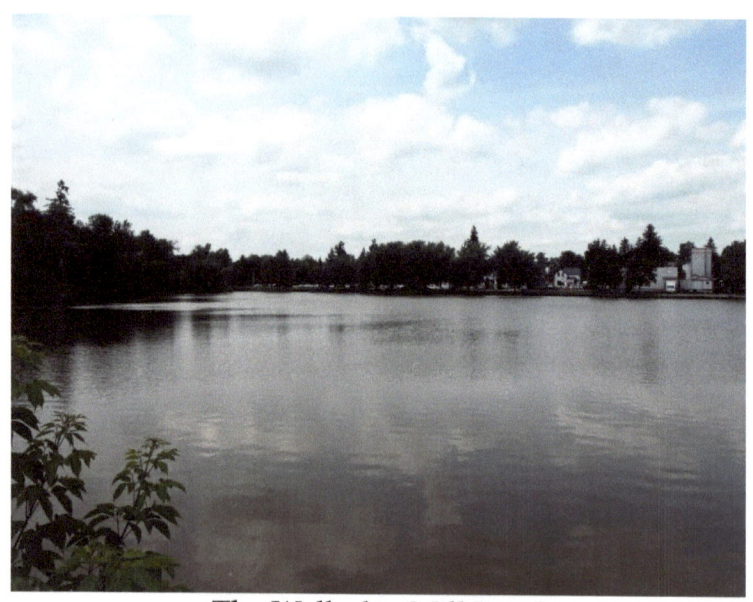

The Wellesley Mill Pond

James Ferris built a saw mill here in 1845 which quickly became the centre of commercial development. John Schmidt developed the area and in 1856 Christopher and Henry Doering built a flour and gristmill. With the coming of steam and electrical power in the 1900s, the Mill Pond was used less for industry and more for recreation such as swimming and fishing. The Doering's mill closed in 1996 and a walking trail was constructed the following year.

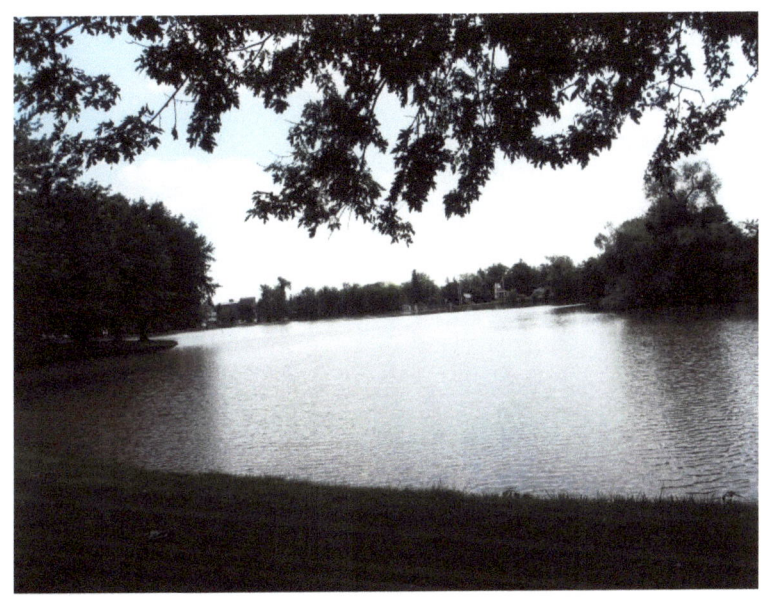

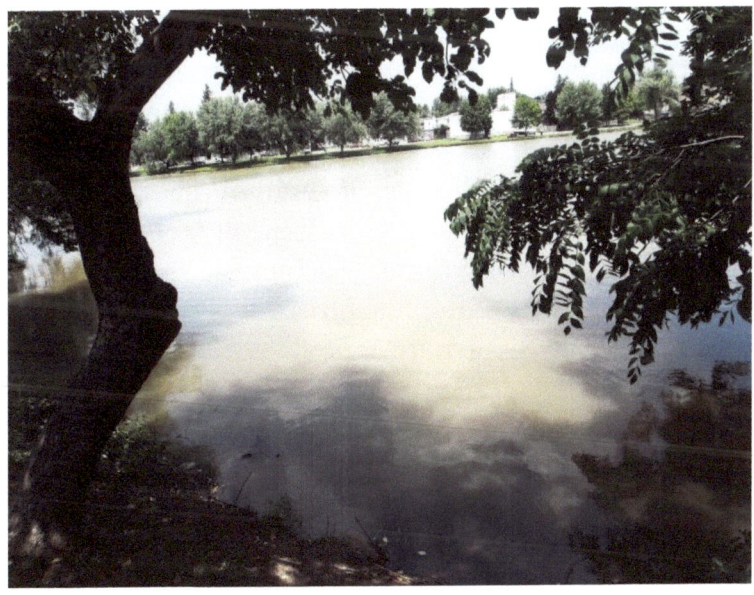

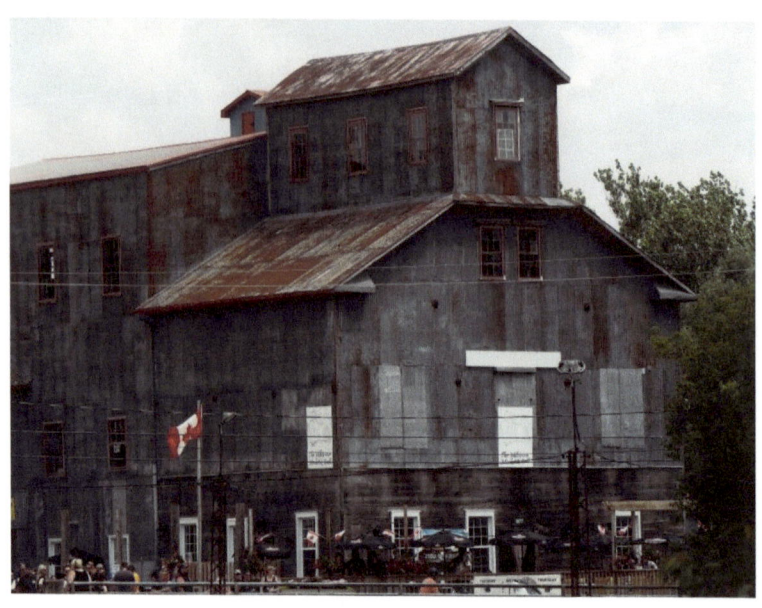

3677 Nafziger Road - Wellesley Mill built in 1856, 1910
Its half-timbered walls are made of massive timber framing
resting on a stone foundation, with brick infilling between the
timbers. The foundation walls range between thirty inches
and three to four feet thick. Remnants of original milling
equipment, including elevators, pulleys and bins, and other
memorabilia from the mill's past are still in place.
Christopher and Henry Doering built the older section of the
mill in 1856. The Doering family also started the first general
store here. The flour milling machinery worked on water
power until the late nineteenth century when it was converted
to steam. The Faber brothers owned the mill in the early 1900s
and added the third storey and the front section in 1910.
When they sold the mill to Jacob Leis in the early 1920s, the
Fabers took much of the flour milling equipment with them to
Tavistock where they established another mill and the
Wellesley Mill became primarily a feed mill.

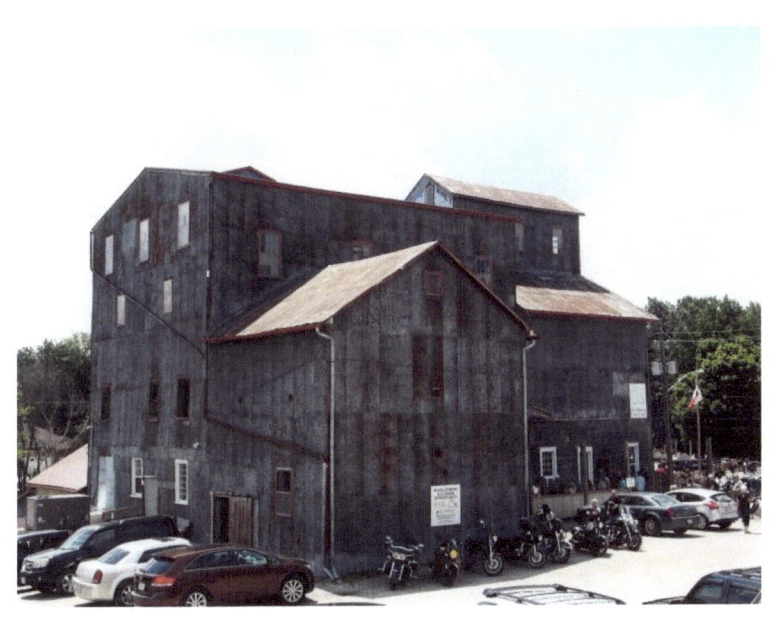

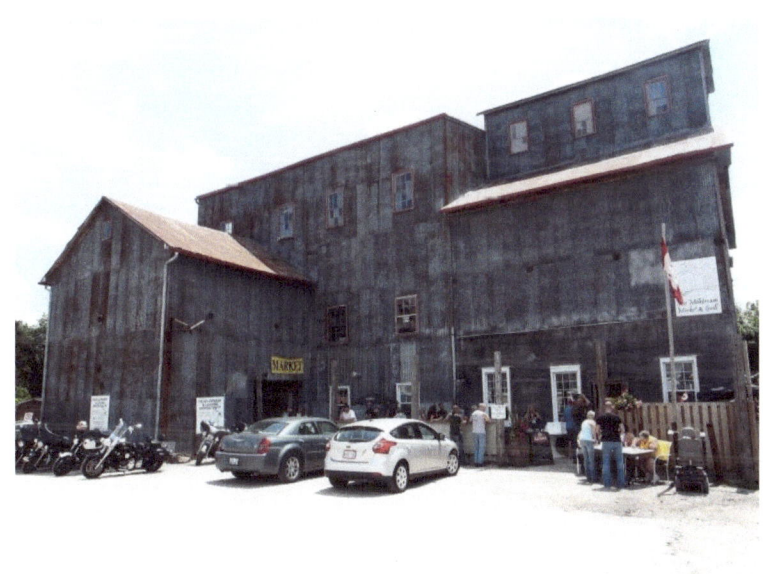

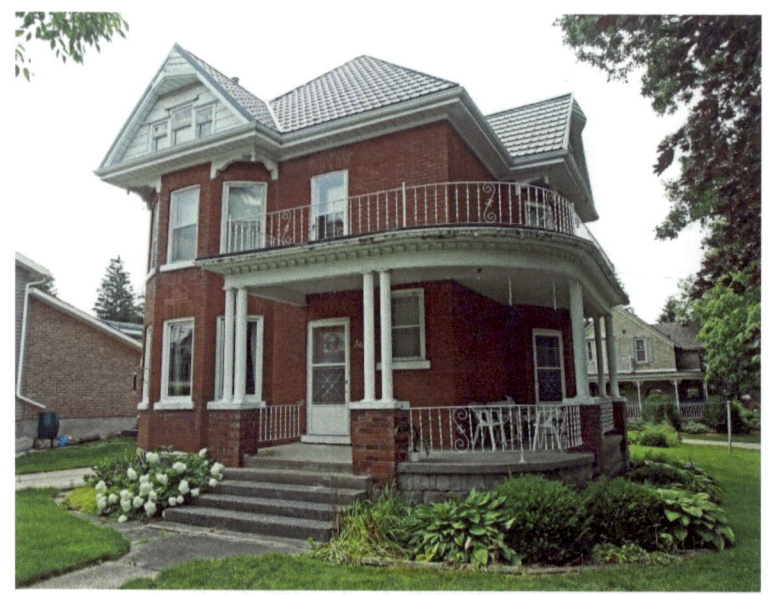

Nafziger Road – Edwardian – wraparound verandahs on both storeys, Palladian window, fretwork

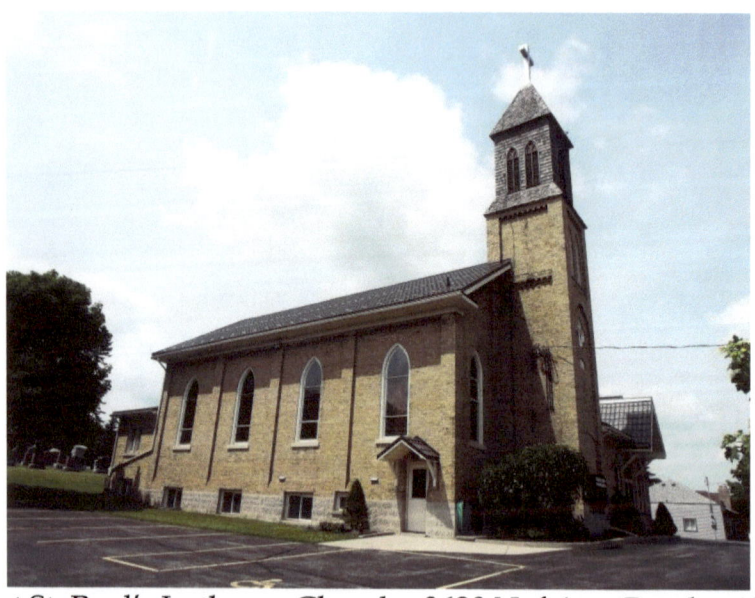

First St. Paul's Lutheran Church - 3620 Nafziger Road c. 1876

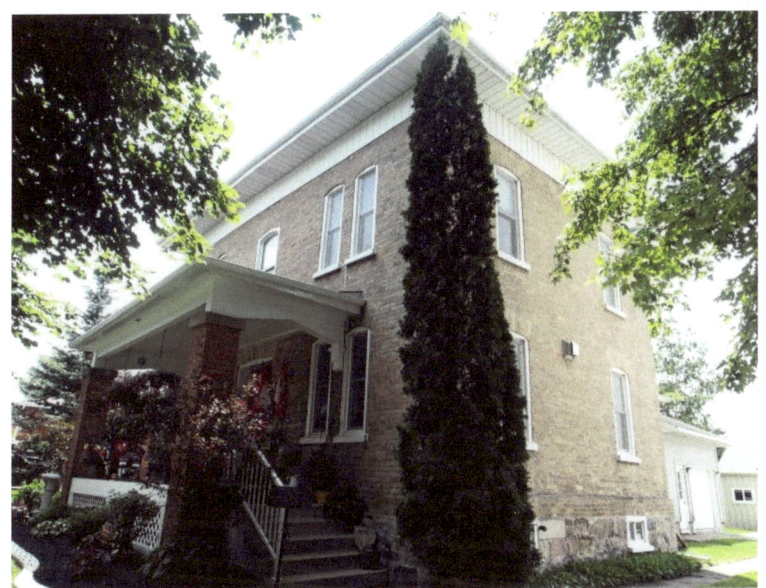

David Street – Italianate – hipped roof

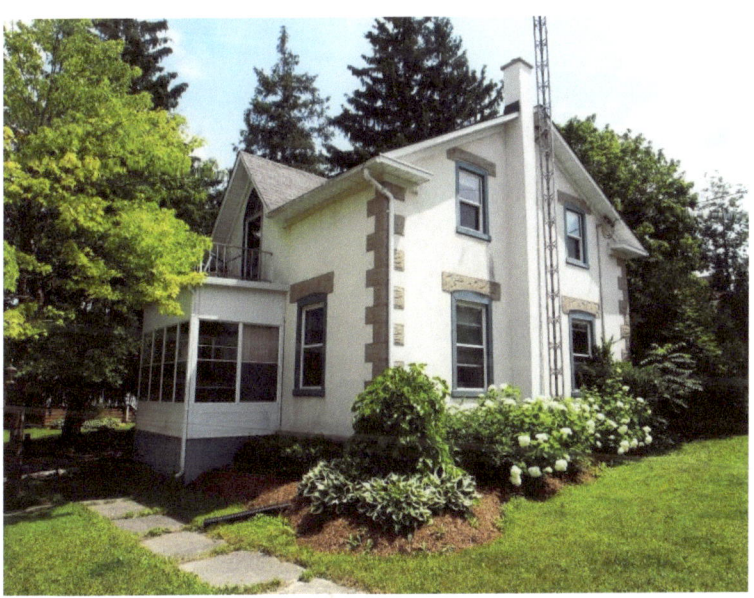

1064 Doering Street – Gothic Revival, corner quoins

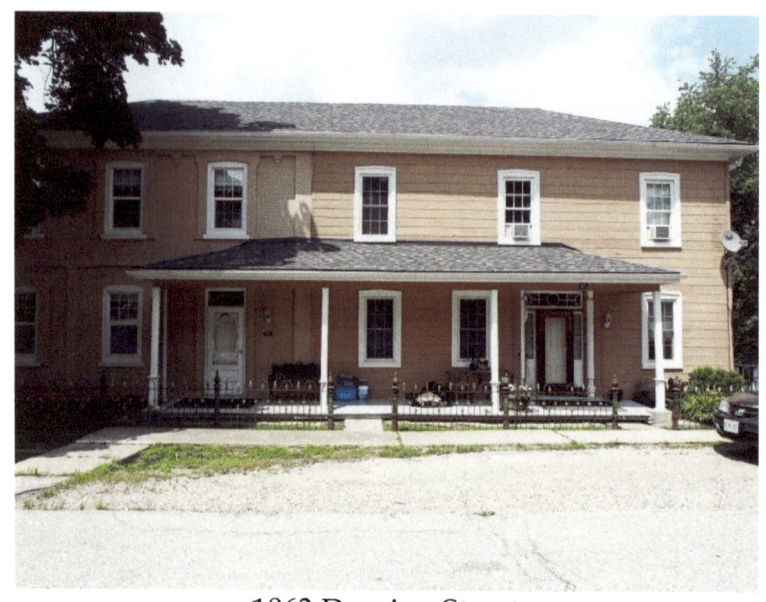

1063 Doering Street

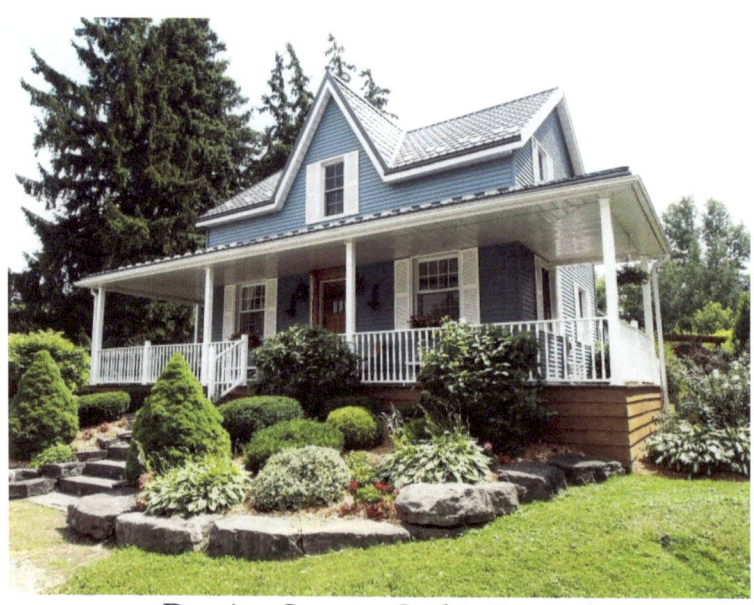

Doering Street – Gothic Revival

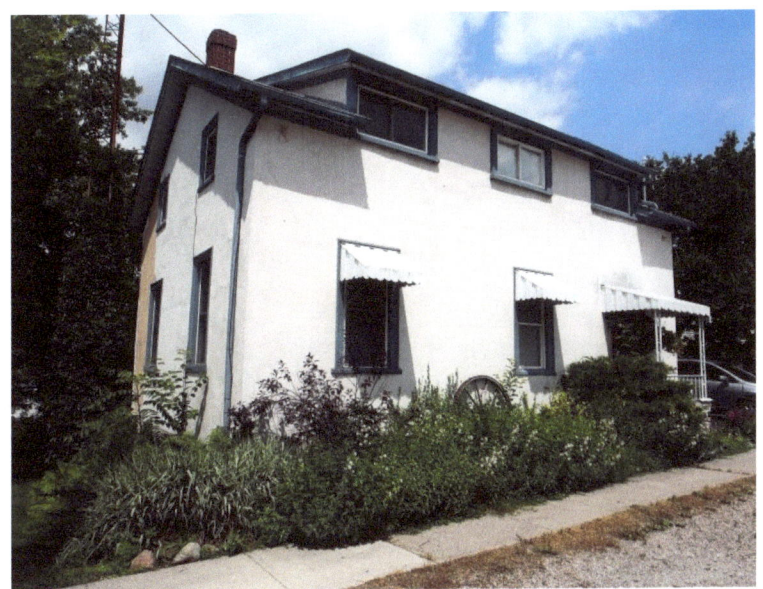

1057 Doering Street – Gothic Revival

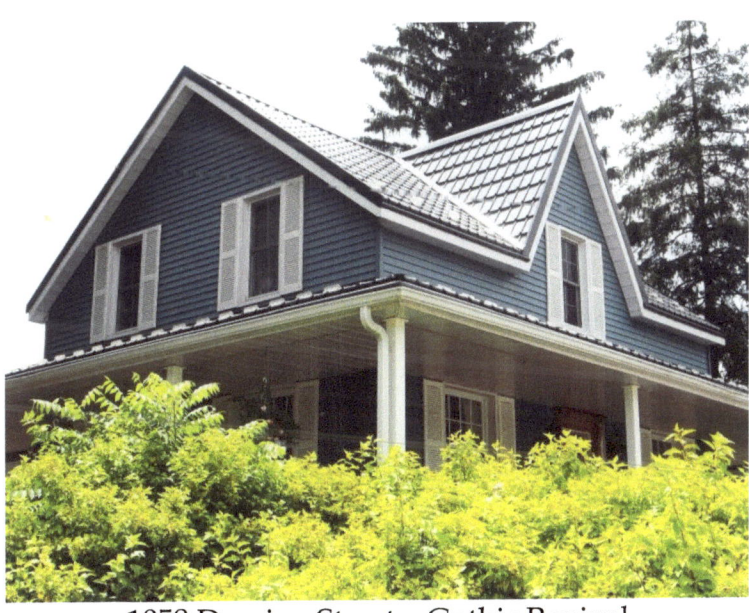

1058 Doering Street – Gothic Revival

Architectural Terms

Brackets: a decorative or weight-bearing structural element which forms a right angle with one side against a wall and the other under a projecting surface such as an eave or roof. Example: 1164 Henry Street	
Cobblestone architecture: Refers to the use of cobblestones embedded in mortar as a method for erecting walls on houses and commercial buildings. Example: 1189 Queen's Bush Road	
Cornice: originally the wooden overhang of the roof. With the use of stone, brick, iron and steel, the cornice is any projecting shelf at the top of a ceiling or roof. They can be very decorative. Example: 1153 Queen's Bush Road	
Cornice Return: decorative element on the end of a gable. Example: 1129 Henry Street	
Dentil Moulding: an even series of rectangles used as ornamental decoration in cornices. Example: 3620 Nafziger Road, First St. Paul's Lutheran Church	

Dormer: (French for "sleep") a gable end window that pierces through the plane of a sloping roof surface to create usable space in the top floor or attic of a building by adding headroom. Example: Queen's Bush Road	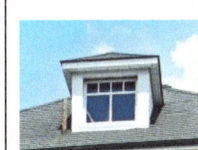
Fretwork: interlaced decorative design resembling a bracket Example: Nafziger Road	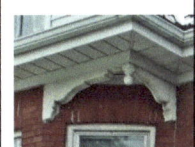
Frontispiece: a portion of the façade of a building, usually a centred doorway that is slightly raised from the rest of the building, usually has extensive ornamentation. Frontispieces are usually Classical in design with white columned porches. Example: Henry Street, Wellesley Township Heritage Historical Society	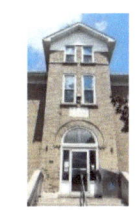
Gable: the triangular portion of a wall between the edges of a sloping roof. Example: Buxton House, Molesworth Street	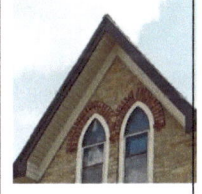

Hipped Roof: a roof where all sides slope downwards to the walls with no gables. Example: 1115 Queen's Bush Road	
Lancet Window: a tall, narrow window with a pointed arch at its top. Example: 3620 Nafziger Road, First St. Paul's Lutheran Church	
Mansard Roof: This style was popularized by Francois Mansart (1598-1666), an accomplished architect of the French Baroque period and especially fashionable during the Second French Empire (1852-1870). This roof is almost flat on the top section, with two slopes on each of its sides with the lower slope at a steeper angle than the upper and having dormer windows. Example: 1193 Queen's Bush Road, Nith River Chop House	
Palladian Window: a large window that is divided into three sections with the centre section larger than the two side sections and usually arched. Example: 1159 Queen's Bush Road, Wellesley	
Pediment: a triangular section above the horizontal structure (entablature), typically supported by columns. The inside of the triangle is called the tympanum. Example: Henry Street	

Quoin: masonry blocks at the corner of a wall, often a decorative feature, usually larger or of a different colour than the rest of the wall. Example: Queen's Bush Road	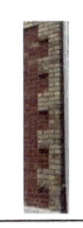
Rose Window: a circular window with ornamental tracery radiating from the centre. Example: 3620 Nafziger Road, First St. Paul's Lutheran Church	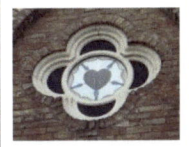
Vergeboard: also called bargeboards – hang from the projecting end of a roof and are often elaborately carved and ornamented. Example: 1140 Queen's Bush Road	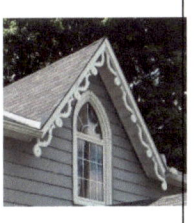

Building Styles

Edwardian, 1900-1930 – This style bridges the ornate and elaborate styles of the Victorian era and the simplified styles of the 20th century. Balanced facades, simple roof lines, dormer windows, large front porches, and smooth brick surfaces are its characteristics. Example: 1159 Queen's Bush Road	
Georgian, before 1860 – This style began with the British King Georges in the 18th century. These buildings have balanced facades around a central door, medium-pitched gable roofs, and small paned windows. Example: 1180 Queen's Bush Road	
Gothic Revival, 1830-1890 – These decorative buildings have sharply-pitched gables with highly detailed vergeboards, pointed-arch window openings, and dichromatic brickwork. It is a common style in Ontario. Example: 1221 Queen's Bush Road	

A log cabin, built from logs, was usually one- or 1½-storeys constructed with round rather than hewn, or hand-worked, logs, and erected quickly for frontier shelter. Log cabins were built from logs laid horizontally and interlocked on the ends with notches. The cabin was situated to provide sunlight and drainage so the pioneers could cope better with the rigors of frontier life. The pioneers chose old-growth trees that were straight and had few knots and did not need to be hewn to fit well together. Careful notching minimized the size of the gap between the logs and reduced the amount of chinking with sticks and rocks or daubing with mud to fill the gap. The length of one log was the length of one wall. Example: 1149 Queen's Bush Road	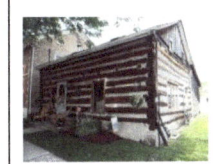
Italianate, 1850-1900 – It has wide-bracketed eaves, belvederes, wrap-around verandahs. Example: 1115 Queen's Bush Road	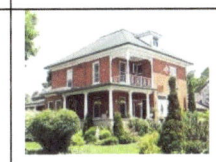
Queen Anne, 1885-1900 – This style is distinguished by an irregular outline featuring a combination of an offset tower, broad gables, projecting two-storey bays, verandahs, multi-sloped roofs, and tall, decorative chimneys. A mixture of brick and wood is common. Windows often have one large single-paned bottom sash and small panes in the upper sash. Example: 1155 Queen's Bush Road	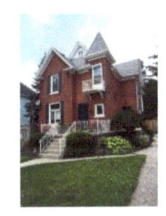

www.ingramcontent.com/pod-product-compliance
Lightning Source LLC
Chambersburg PA
CBHW040921180526
45159CB00002BA/562